THE
NEWCASTLE
RUGBY STORY

THE
NEWCASTLE
RUGBY STORY

Alan Hedley

TEMPUS

First published 2000

PUBLISHED IN THE UNITED KINGDOM BY:

Tempus Publishing Ltd
The Mill, Brimscombe Port
Stroud, Gloucestershire GL5 2QG

PUBLISHED IN THE UNITED STATES OF AMERICA BY:

Tempus Publishing Inc.
2A Cumberland Street
Charleston, SC 29401

Tempus books are available in France, Germany and Belgium
from the following addresses:

Tempus Publishing Group	Tempus Publishing Group	Tempus Publishing Group
21 Avenue de la République	Gustav-Adolf-Straße 3	Place de L'Alma 4/5
37300 Joué-lès-Tours	99084 Erfurt	1200 Brussels
FRANCE	GERMANY	BELGIUM

British Library Cataloguing in Publication Data.
A catalogue record for this book is available from the British Library.

ISBN 0 7524 2046 1

Typesetting and origination by Tempus Publishing.
PRINTED AND BOUND IN GREAT BRITAIN.

CONTENTS

ACKNOWLEDGEMENTS

Where do I start? There are so many people who have helped me with the writing of this book, which has been a very rewarding experience, although at times I wondered what on earth I was doing – but then I have the impression most people wonder what on earth I'm doing most of the time anyway.

First of all, I'd like to thank my wife Sandra for her support and encouragement, for the endless cups of coffee and for taking on the task of reading the text and preventing the many howlers I initially made.

My thanks also go to my employers, the *Newcastle Chronicle and Journal*, for granting permission for the writing of this book and the use of photographs. An acknowledgement is also due to North News and Pictures, Gosforth FC and Trevor Hogg for their help with photographs and also Newcastle Falcons for permission to use their logo and information from their records and programme publications.

Thanks also go to Duncan Madsen and Ken Lockerbie for their help on matters of fact and historical accuracy and, again, Trevor Hogg for his help in compiling records, which proved a far more difficult task than anyone could imagine because of their fragmentary nature. I'd also like to thank James Howarth of Tempus Publishing for coming up with the idea of the book and for his patience when I missed several deadlines. Most of all, I'd like to thank the players and officials of Gosforth, Newcastle Gosforth and Newcastle Falcons down the years who have given me more fun and more good times than they can possibly imagine.

Sport, especially professional sport, is a serious business these days but rugby seems to be able to retain a sense of humour and be able to laugh at itself. The Newcastle club have always had that ability more than most and long may that continue.

FOREWORD

by Rob Andrew

Five years ago I was given the unique opportunity of being in on the ground floor of professional rugby with Newcastle Falcons. When Sir John Hall's Sporting Club assumed control of Gosforth it was a bold, exciting venture. It still is.

In those five years, which have seen this famous club transformed from Newcastle Gosforth into the Falcons, it's been a real roller-coaster ride with exhilarating peaks and some excruciating troughs but I would not have missed it for the world and, I suspect, neither would Alan Hedley, the author of this book.

A respected journalist for twenty-five years on both the national and North East rugby scene, Alan has covered this club through the glory years of the 1970s, the lean years that followed and the climb back to national prominence. He has watched the transformation from Gosforth to Newcastle Gosforth to Newcastle Falcons and has been a witness to every twist and turn, every crisis and every triumph and I suspect he has watched, with a certain amount of glee at times, as the Falcons became a real force in English rugby.

He has had, and still has, a unique and a privileged seat ringside and will admit, if pushed, that sometimes he has been even closer to the action than he should have been. Sometimes too close for his own comfort, as he almost got himself arrested one night with the rest of the Gosforth team in Gloucester! That's a story you won't find in this book because, in the best traditions of 'what happens on tour stays on tour' or perhaps in the best interests of self-preservation, Alan won't reveal what happened that night. Not in this book anyway; perhaps one day he might, provided he changes the names to protect the guilty!

What will be found in this book is a comprehensive history of the Newcastle club which celebrates its 125th anniversary in two years' time. It's the story of how Gosforth became a national force, how the club which scaled the heights in the 1970s with a John Player Cup double then plumbed the depths in the late 1980s and early 1990s, before being transformed with the advent of professionalism and the birth of the Falcons.

The putting together of a professional side from scratch, avoiding relegation from Division Two in the first season, achieving promotion and then winning the Premiership title in the first season in the top flight would de dismissed as wild fiction if it wasn't perfectly true. If someone either decides to update this book or publish a commemoration of the 150th or 200th anniversary of the Newcastle club, as I'm sure they will, there will be much, much more to add to the list of honours.

Rob Andrew
Director of Rugby
Newcastle RFC

INTRODUCTION

The rise of Newcastle Falcons to the top of English rugby in the space of five years is a remarkable story, but there is more to it than that. The Falcons did not appear out of nowhere to win the Allied Dunbar Premiership, although it may seem like that to many. Neither did they buy their way to the championship with Sir John Hall's millions, though many scoff at the title-winning Newcastle side of 1978 as mercenaries.

It's true that Sir John Hall's chequebook enabled Rob Andrew to put together a side capable of winning the Premiership but you need more than mercenaries to win titles, you need a team and that's what the Falcons became. In doing so they restored pride to Gosforth, a once-great club who had been in danger of sliding into oblivion, and revived interest in Rugby Union in the North-East. The triumph also proved that sports-mad Geordies will get behind their team given the chance.

Gosforth's early years were unremarkable, but they exploded onto the national scene in the 1970s, winning two John Player Cups and becoming the most feared side in the land. Just when it seemed they were a spent force in the 1990s professionalism, Sir John Hall and Rob Andrew came along to transform a moribund club into national champions.

Little did those young men realise what they were starting when they met in a summer house in 1877 to form Gosforth Football Club. It was the beginning of a fascinating history, one packed with trials, tribulations and triumphs, with success and near disaster as the club almost folded at least half a dozen times during its lifetime.

Each time the club has survived these threats and grown stronger. The signs are that the club will be part of the North-East and national sporting scene for many more years to come.

1
IN THE BEGINNING

Newcastle Falcons are viewed as relative newcomers, perhaps even upstarts, by the rugby establishment. Indeed, if you adhere to the strictest definition they are, having been formed as a result of Sir John Hall's takeover of Newcastle Gosforth in 1995. However, contrary to the belief in some quarters, the Tyneside club is not the bastard child of professionalism, born when the International Board declared the game of Rugby Union open. When the IB opened the floodgates of professionalism at their special meeting in Paris on 26 August 1995, it was a date as significant in the history of the Newcastle club as 1877, the year of the birth of the Gosforth club.

It was as Gosforth that the Newcastle club started life and they can trace their lineage through a long history before metamorphosing into Newcastle Gosforth and, ultimately, the Falcons. Gosforth was formed at a meeting held in the summer house at No. 1 Gosforth Villas, High Street, Gosforth, the home of W. Farr, and was attended by a number of boys and ex-pupils from Durham School, who even today have a strong link with the Newcastle club. The object of the meeting was to form a rugby club in Gosforth and after some discussion Gosforth Football Club was born. Unfortunately, the exact date of the meeting is not recorded, but it must have been in September or October 1877 because the new club played its first game on 3 November of that year.

As many of those involved in the meeting still possessed the Durham School jersey of green and white hoops, it was decided to adopt these as the club colours. This continued to be so for many years until the team's colours were changed to black and white when the club became part of Sir John Hall's Newcastle Sporting Club.

The first match involving the new Gosforth club was played on 3 November 1877 and it was against Northern, who had been formed as Elswick in 1876 but changed their name to Northern in 1877. Northern were to become arguably the leading side in Northumberland, following the decline of Rockcliff and Percy Park and were still pre-eminent until Gosforth's emergence in the 1970s as England's top club. Again, there is no record of where the game was played but it is more than likely that it was on either the County Cricket ground in Northumberland Road, South Northumberland Cricket Ground or Ashburton Meadows.

This first match planted the seed which was to grow into intense rivalry between the two clubs in later years. The rivalry was often bitter, petty and stupid, but also enthralling as they knocked seven bells out of each other in their annual Boxing Day derbies.

The match in 1877 saw Gosforth take the field very much as the new boys, although they did not perform too badly. A report appeared in the *Newcastle Chronicle* from 5 November 1877 and an extract reads: 'Gosforth is a new club, this being its first match, but the whole of their team played exceedingly well and amongst them W. Gillies and M. Fenwick may be mentioned as distinguishing themselves. From Northern, A. Cadle made some splendid runs and G. Mason and W. Kyall did good work. The match ended in a draw in favour of Northern. Each side scored a try, though Gosforth had to touch down four times in self-defence. S.F. Bates scored for Gosforth and C. Gibson for Northern.'

Records from the first few seasons are fragmentary but it is known that S.F. Bates was the club's first secretary, W.S. Williams the first captain and Revd Allan Charlton the club president. The club played their matches on a ground at Ashburton Meadows, to the west end of Gosforth. In the season following formation, games were played against North Durham, Tynemouth, Northern, College of Physical Science, Westoe, Houghton-le-Spring, Accountants, Northumberland (a club side not to be confused with Northumberland County) and Bank Clerks.

Five years later Gosforth amalgamated with the Northumberland club as both had lost their grounds because of building work. Apparently, there was a heated argument before the name Northumberland was adopted because they were the senior side by some five years. Northumberland was the original name of the club created by the premiumed apprentices of the Armstrong Whitworth factory in 1872 and it was the first team formed in the county. A combined practice match took place at the beginning of the season on the South Northumberland cricket ground.

The combined club played that season as Northumberland Rugby Football Club at the South Northumberland ground behind Gosforth High Street. The move from Ashburton Meadows to the South Northumberland ground and the merger was the first instance of the precarious and nomadic history of the Gosforth club, which remained with them right into the 1990s. Nevertheless, in 1887 the combined club changed its name to that of Gosforth Rugby Football Club and moved to another new ground at Regent Road.

Northumberland continued on their own until 1892, when they disbanded, and two years later Gosforth were facing the same possibility after severe financial problems surfaced. However, it was decided to sell the club's goalposts (just about their only asset as they did not own their ground or a clubhouse) to a group of players who called themselves Gosforth Nomads. The club continued as a junior side, playing when and where they could – presumably taking their posts with them!

In 1898 there was a change in playing fortunes and the club showed a steady improvement until they won the Northumberland and Durham Second Teams Competition in 1905/06, which meant they were raised to senior status the following season. From that point the club was firmly established, both on and off the field, but they still had no ground to call their own and continued a nomadic existence which was to last until the 1950s, playing on various sites including the Northumberland County Ground.

During the First World War a heavy price was paid and twenty-six Gosforth members lost their lives. The club reformed in September 1919 and the first game was played against Old Novos on the Newcastle Royal Grammar School ground. The team was made up of players who had mainly just returned from military service and included A.M. Smallwood, who later became an England international, E.C. Kinghorn, W. Dixon, W. Armstrong, T. Young, Ralph Worthington, Bob Allan, who also had England trials, and D.C. Davies.

The club shared the Northumberland County Ground (now the site of a supermarket) with Northern and each had home games on alternate Saturdays –

The first known picture of a Gosforth side is the Gosforth Nomads team of 1906/07. They achieved senior status the previous season by winning the Northumberland and Durham Second Teams Cup. The team is from left to right, back row: J.A. Robinson (team secretary), T.C. Thompson, J. Graham, S. Atkinson, A.E. March, J. Smith, G.J. March, J.R. Lunn, R.J. Lawson (secretary). Middle row: J.P. Lunn, G.W. Foreman, W.D. Kinnis, H.O. Robinson (captain), R. Crow, G. Bell, H. Welford (referee). Front row: H.R. Potts, R. Richardson, E.W. Hood.

possibly the only time the two clubs have agreed on anything! The ground was situated opposite what is now the Regent Centre Metro station. H.T. Robinson was secretary and the three Robinson brothers, H.O., Angus and R.M., were very much the heart of the club along with groundsman Bob Trotter who also doubled as coach-trainer. There were changing facilities and one normal-sized domestic bath for all the players to share and, as there was no licence for the sale of beer, the County Hotel in Gosforth was the favourite haunt of the players. It still is a regular venue for the area's rugby players today.

The Douglas or the Eldon pubs in Newcastle were also used, but the weekly selection meetings were held in the County. An indication that the club was very well established was the fact that games were played against all the local clubs, although games were played no further afield than Hartlepool. There was also no scheduled training session, this was left to the individual.

The playing field that adjoined the Northumberland County Ground was used for second and third team games, indicating the growing strength of the club. The third team won the Northumberland Third Teams Cup in 1921, but seven years later Gosforth showed that they had really arrived when they won the Northumberland Senior Cup for the first time by beating Percy Park 5-3 in the final. Gosforth were cup finalists again in 1932, losing 19-8 to Seghill, and 1936, losing 23-21 to Tynedale in what was said to be one of the most exciting cup finals ever seen.

This is the Gosforth team that won the club's first Northumberland Cup in 1928. From left to right, back row: L. Patterson, J.W. Lindsay, A.K. Martin, E. Dunford, S.H. Bowes, J.A. Baty, S.G. March, R.M. Robinson (president). Middle row: F. Hoult, F.W. Morrison, J.H. Bordas, D.C. Punter, S.M. Carter, W. Wearmouth. Front row: G.S. Bowerbank, W.R. Doig.

In 1937, the club celebrated its diamond jubilee and a dinner organised by Mr A.R. Glenton was held on 4 December. An England trial had taken place that afternoon at the County Ground and both teams were invited to the dinner along with the president of the Rugby Football Union, Major-General B.A. Hill, CB, DSO. Also present were many well-known rugby personalities including Carston Catcheside, club chairman H.O. Robinson, club president G.P. Taylor, Bob Oakes and G.C. 'Tot' Robinson who, it was said, would have been the club's first England cap in 1897 had he not been ordered by the Northumberland County selectors to move to Percy Park when Gosforth lost their senior status in 1894.

Although progress had been good and the club was well established, the Second World War brought any more advancement to a halt and, apart from the odd game, no rugby was played for six years. After the war Leslie Baty, Walter Doig, who had been secretary for many years and several others set about re-forming a playing side for the 1945/46 season. It wasn't easy but they managed to maintain a side throughout the season and, had they not been successful in getting Gosforth up and running again, it's possible the club may never have been revived.

2
NEW GROUND

As more Gosforth members returned from the forces, the club turned its attention to the question of a ground of its own and, with the princely sum of £48 in the ground fund, it was decided to pursue that course. Not for the first time Gosforth took the plunge without really knowing what was under the surface. To try and raise money in a time when belts were being tightened all round seemed the height of folly, but under the driving force of Martin Millican many fund-raising schemes were started and they regularly brought in around £1,000 a year until, amazingly, there was £10,000 in the kitty.

In 1951, after many sites had been looked at and rejected, twelve acres of land on the west side of the Great North Road were purchased. Those who bought the land at the time could not have realised just how important their choice would be in the future, when the club was able to sell the ground to a builder for more than £1 million and relocate to Kingston Park. There they would build one of the finest playing surfaces in the country. However, The New Ground as it was to be called, certainly could not be called a good

Doug Smith (with ball) captained Gosforth to their fourth Northumberland County Cup final in 1950, albeit unsuccessfully as they lost 9-3 to Percy Park. They also lost 9-0 to Park the following season and it wasn't until 1956 that they won the cup for the second time. From left to right, back row: F. Stephenson, T. Bird, J. Fryer, R. Gardner, E. Hattam, W.F.M. Hudson, R.B. Fawcett, I.R. Hornsby. Front row: K. Turnbull, C. Ford, H.L. Carey, D. Smith, W.A. Hedley, W.S. Smith, D. Hogg.

A cartoon showing the Gosforth members involved in work to level their new ground in the 1950s.

playing surface as it was a mixture of rubbish tip and market garden and 92,000 tons of earth had to be moved before the site even looked like a playing field. It cost £3,225, which was a large chunk of the ground fund, and the cost of shifting the earth would have been prohibitive. Fortunately, local engineering company Vickers was producing a new tractor from their tank design section and needed somewhere to test their prototype. They were persuaded to try it at Gosforth and the whole earth-moving operation cost the club nothing. The result was that the club had three pitches to use.

If that hurdle was relatively easy to clear, the next one, that of building the clubhouse was not and it was 1954 before the foundation stone was laid by Leslie Baty, the club chairman. When the ground was opened by Joe Brunton, president of the Rugby Union, in September 1955, Gosforth also had a two-storey clubhouse and a stand.

The eventual completion of the ground sparked the club into action, winning the Northumberland Cup for only the second time in their history in 1956 with the Smith brothers, Johnnie, Douglas and Norman, in the side. Douglas was later to become the club's patron. It can be said that Gosforth were well and truly established with the opening of their new ground and clubhouse but, while the club's seventy-fifth anniversary had been celebrated in 1952, it is fair to say that Gosforth were just an ordinary, run-of-the-mill rugby club; no different from hundreds of others.

However, things were changing and within two years of that seventy-fifth anniversary celebration, the fixture list contained games against Harlequins, Blackheath, Rosslyn Park, Oxford Greyhounds and Cambridge University. The arrival of Arthur Smith, who won 4 Cambridge blues from 1954 to 1957, to complete a Ph.D. at Newcastle University, was to

Gosforth's 1956 Northumberland Cup-winning side included the three Smith brothers: Douglas, Johnny and Norman. From left to right, back row: M.S. Vernon, B. Howstan, R. Hollings, D. Bradbeer, K. Richardson, D.F. Kay, G.N. Smith, D. Crawshaw, J.P. Sturgeon, B.J.G. de Zwaan, E.C. Hilton (president). Middle row: D. Smith, J. Fenwick, J.M. Smith, W. Charlton, M.A. Pearey. Front row: W.H. Swales, F. Armstrong, T. Bourn.

Scottish international wing Arthur Smith, who toured twice with the British Lions, was said to be one of the finest players to wear the Gosforth shirt in the 1950s and '60s.

Gosforth's third win in the Northumberland Cup in 1960 was the culmination of an impressive season in which the Nomads won the Northumberland Junior Shield and the club also won the Northumberland County Sevens. This team photograph shows the Northumberland Cup winners, from left to right, back row: J.R. Veitch (secretary), D.R.B. Johnson, J. Guthrie, J.H.B. Coker, D.H. Campbell, J.M. Smith, T.B. Begg, D.R. McIntyre, A. Thompson. Middle row: J.J. Fenwick, K.T. Richardson, E.W. Hoult, B.J.G. de Zwann (captain), R. Pearson (president), F. Armstrong, W. Charlton. Front row: G.S. Blackett, J.P. Sturgeon. Inset: G.N. Smith.

Gosforth celebrated their highly successful 1960 season with a dinner in Tilley's Restaurant. The brochure included photographs of the 1928 and 1956 county cup-winning sides as well as the 1960 Gosforth line-up and the Nomads who won the Northumberland Junior Cup. At the dinner were several county officials including, from left to right: D. Brown (international referee), J.A. Craven (King's College captain), A. Brogden (county president), B. de Zwaan (Gosforth captain), D. Yorke (Gosforth), Sir Lawrie Edwards (Northumberland secretary), R. Wood (Gosforth), and R. Pearson (Gosforth president).

help transform the thinking and attitude of the Gosforth club. Smith won 33 Scotland caps and went on 2 British Lions tours, captaining the 1962 side to South Africa, and was reckoned by many to be the finest wing there has even been, with remarkable acceleration, devastating finishing and an uncanny sense of positioning. Those who saw him play still talk about the cross-kicks that Gordon Blackett – another player who had a huge influence on Gosforth's climb to pre-eminence – would deliver to Smith for the seemingly inevitable try. Ireland's British Lions prop Ray McLoughlin was another player who came to Newcastle University to do his Ph.D. and he, too, had an enormous influence on Gosforth during the mid-1960s.

Players like Smith and McLoughlin could only do so much and the real crux of Gosforth's climb to the top in the 1970s came through the ceaseless work to improve the fixture list from former Northumberland County hooker John Fenwick and then Barry de Zwaan, a former club captain, and Norman Douglas. Johnny Smith was to carry on the task and Tommy Hall continued the role right into the professional era until the fixtures became centralised and controlled by the league structure.

Tommy Hall was a player of some stature in the 1950s and '60s as a flanker of real quality. He played for the North-East Counties and also had the astonishing record of

British Lions and Irish prop Ray McLoughlin was another player who came to Newcastle to complete his Ph.D. and his influence on Gosforth's forward play was immense.

Tommy Hall is presented with the Northumberland Cup by Percy Bates, the Northumberland county president, after Gosforth beat Northern 9-3 in a replay.

19

Gosforth captain Bill Charlton receives the Northumberland County Cup from Jack Spark, president of Northumberland, after Gosforth had beaten Morpeth 16-0 in the final.

playing 50 consecutive county championship games for Northumberland and, taking friendly matches into account, it was probably nearer 60.

The steady improvement in fixtures and quality of player was underlined in 1968 when the club won all four Northumberland County Cups and the County Colts Sevens. Bill Charlton, who was captain of Gosforth in 1962/63, was also the first rugby master at Gosforth Grammar School (now Gosforth High School) and he was instrumental in sending many ready-made players into the green and white hoops in the 1960s. There was also the influence of players like Gordon Blackett, an unconventional and brilliant fly-half who eventually went to Rugby League and was followed by his scrum-half partner Brian Gascoigne (both went to Huddersfield). England trialist prop Ken Richardson and Ray McLoughlin were also important figures. When it seemed that the impetus such players had given the club would fizzle out, players of the quality of Malcolm Young, Duncan Madsen, Roger Uttley, David Robinson and Peter Dixon all came to the club towards the end of the 1960s and the beginning of the 1970s. This led to Gosforth moving forward from dominating rugby in the North-East to assuming a similar position on a national level by the mid-1970s.

3
GLORY DAYS

Gosforth's climb to the top of rugby's tree in the 1970s and 1980s was based on the quality of their players and their strength in depth. It wasn't just the triumvirate of Uttley, Dixon and Robinson. Players such as the Patrick brothers Harry and Brian, who was an England trialist at the age of seventeen, Terry Roberts, Richard Breakey, John Hedley, Colin White, Steve Gustard and Kenny Britton, arguably the best uncapped centre in England during that period, gave Gosforth an edge other sides in the North-East could only dream about and national sides learned to fear.

Malcolm Young joined the club from Tynedale – he had won a blue at Cambridge playing soccer, after switching from rugby because he had broken a wrist! It was Young's partnership with the back row of Roger Uttley, Peter Dixon and David Robinson that provided another piece of the jigsaw.

Roger Uttley arrived at Gosforth after coming to the North-East to study for his teaching diploma at Ponteland and stayed on. In the 1970s, he was the most instantly

Malcolm Young in action in a 1970s match. This was the start of Young's glittering career with the green and whites.

recognisable rugby figure in both the North-East and England and he went on to captain his country and play for the British Lions. Uttley would also become England coach and manager and British Lions forwards coach.

Peter Dixon won 4 blues for Oxford and many class him as the best back row forward ever to play for England, although the Lions recognised it first and capped him before his country did. He scored the only try in the Test against the All Blacks at Auckland in 1971, which enabled the Lions to win the series 2-1 and his arrival at Gosforth after taking up a post at Durham University was probably one of the most fortunate things that ever happened to the club.

If the arrival of Dixon and Uttley was fortuitous, that of David Robinson was the icing on the cake. Robinson, who played for England in two internationals against Japan in 1971 (for which no caps were awarded), also played for the Barbarians and should have been a fixture in the England back row – he was the Neil Back of his time. He is still a legend in Cumbria from the days when he played county rugby for what was then called Cumberland and Westmoreland. After two seasons with Birkenhead Park, Robinson decided he was better off playing in a pack that would give his talents as an offensive flanker their full rein. His two tries in two minutes in the 1977 John Player Cup final turned that game in Gosforth's favour. It was a feat he repeated many times.

The relationship between Jack Rowell as coach and Robinson as captain was one of the finest in the club's history, and led directly to Gosforth's mid-1970s surge and their first John Player Cup triumph. Rowell was to go on to further glory as coach to Bath and England and he still retains a link with the club as honorary president of the Newcastle Falcons Supporters Club.

The back row of the scrum loses most of its effectiveness unless the front five is at least able to hold its own and Gosforth were again fortunate to have players of quality in the second and front row. In Duncan Madsen, Gosforth unearthed a hooker of real quality who played for Scotland and the Barbarians. Now a journalist but previously a solicitor, he freely admits some of the things he got up to on the field would be pretty indefensible even by the most persuasive lawyer. However, along with Andy Cutter and Colin White, his rugged and uncompromising approach was vital to survival in the jungle warfare that was normal among the forwards in club rugby at that time.

Jack Rowell, who captained the side in 1971/72, became the club's first coach and led them to their first national triumph (the 1976 John Player Cup) before moving on to Bath and England. He was succeeded in 1977 by Mike Mahoney, who was to have three spells as club coach and was synonymous with the club right up to the 1990s. It was during Rowell's year of captaincy that the club won the Telegraph Pennant – there were no leagues or Premiership as there is today – and enjoyed a run of 20 successive victories.

Gosforth dominated The Journal Trophy, a merit table based on North-East clubs and run by the local morning paper. For many years it was the only measure of a club's success in the North-East, along with the Sunday Telegraph Pennant in the North, before regional and then national merit tables came along, initially as a means to decide the qualification for the RFU Knock-Out Cup, which became known as the John Player Cup, then the Pilkington Cup and now the Tetley's Bitter Cup. The national merit table

The 1971/72 season was another great one for Gosforth. They won the Sunday Telegraph Pennant as the top side in the North and retained the Northumberland County Cup. The side contained future England manager Jack Rowell (with cup), who was to become club coach; Duncan Madsen (holding pennant, second from left on front row), who went to play hooker for Scotland; Malcolm Young (on end of front row) and Roger Uttley (middle of back row), who would play together for England; and Mike Mahoney (third from left on back row), who would become the club's coach and first Director of Rugby.

was the forerunner of the national leagues, which Courage and then Allied Dunbar sponsored.

The Premiership is now the main competition but the John Player Cup became the pre-eminent competition of the 1970s. By winning it twice in 1976 and 1977, Gosforth could rightly lay claim to be the country's top club side but in 1971/72, despite winning the Sunday Telegraph Pennant by finishing top of twenty-two northern clubs, Gosforth went out in the first round of the cup 13-9 at Halifax. They won 31 of their 39 games in the 1971/72 season and with Jack Rowell and South African-born Barry de Zwann the driving force off the field, the quality of the side and the quality of fixtures continued to improve. There were matches against sides such as Coventry, Bedford, Headingley, Met Police, Liverpool, Sale, Richmond, Waterloo, Rosslyn Park, Wilmslow as well as local clubs Morpeth, Novos, Tynedale, Newcastle University, Darlington, Sunderland, Percy Park and Hartlepool Rovers.

Ten of the Gosforth side played for Northumberland County and the club won the Northumberland Cup and the Northumberland Sevens, while Roger Uttley toured with England to the Far East and Peter Dixon and Ray McLoughlin had gone to New Zealand with the British Lions. Dixon, at that time, was playing for Harlequins while McLoughlin was still in Ireland with Blackrock College but both were to join Gosforth and add to the growing forward strength.

Duncan Madsen took over as captain of the club in 1972/73 and while the season was not quite as successful with 19 out of 42 games lost, the Northumberland Cup was

Malcolm Young ended up in the Guinness Book of Records *after scoring an individual record for a club game of 37 points in the 53-3 win over Waterloo with 4 tries, 6 conversions and 3 penalties. A try in those days was worth 4 points.*

retained. Malcolm Young scored 423 points and Brian Patrick arrived on the scene at full-back while still at school and played for England Under-19s and also in the full England trial.

Dave Robinson, known universally as Robbo, was skipper in 1973/74, when 31 games out of 39 were won. It was a terrific season, with Gosforth topping the unofficial Northern merit table and Roger Uttley and Peter Dixon playing for England and Duncan Madsen for Scotland. Dave Robinson also played for the Barbarians and wing David Carr had England trials. David Carr, David Robinson, Malcolm Young, Brian Patrick and Colin White all also played for the North against Australia.

David Robinson was elected captain again for 1974/75 and another impressive season saw only 6 games lost and 2 drawn out of the 38 that were played. Gosforth were the North's top club again, retaining the Northumberland Cup and making their first serious run at the John Player Cup before losing in the quarter-finals at Bedford 12-6. Duncan Madsen, Peter Dixon and Roger Uttley played for their respective countries in the Five Nations Championship and Colin White had a final England trial. Young continued his phenomenal form with the boot, scoring 350 points, and Steve Gustard clocked up 20 tries on the wing.

This was the real start of Gosforth's golden period and when Uttley succeeded Robinson as captain, the club became the first Northern side to win the John Player Cup in 1975/76, although Uttley had the disappointment of missing the final triumph because of injury. The season was a great one as Gosforth won 36 of their 42 games and scored 1,165 points, winger Steve Gustard bagged a record 42 tries and Malcolm Young rattled up a record 455 points as the club won the Northumberland Cup for the seventh successive year. Duncan Madsen was in the Scotland team at hooker, Peter Dixon was recalled to the England side and Uttley

Roger Uttley (far left), Peter Dixon (next left) and John Hedley (centre) with Colin White (right) battle it out with the Tynedale forwards on their way to winning the 1975 Northumberland Cup final.

Back row David Robinson doing what he did best – getting the ball away from a maul – in the Gosforth versus Tynedale 1975 Northumberland Cup final.

Gosforth wing Roger Biggs attacks the Tynedale defence in the 1975 Northumberland Cup final.

would have been as well had he not broken a leg. That injury kept him out of the John Player Cup final and Young captained the side to a 23-14 win over Rosslyn Park in front of a disappointing crowd of only 7,500. Unfortunately, the Middlesex Sevens clashed with the final and certainly didn't help the attendance.

To get to the final, Gosforth had survived a rugged semi-final with Sale. Ten minutes from time, England prop Fran Cotton was sent off for throwing a punch at Malcolm Young. Gosforth won the tie 12-3 to set up their first visit to a Twickenham final against Rosslyn Park, who were clear favourites as they were the strongest side in London at the time. The fact that Gosforth were without Roger Uttley was seen by many pundits as a decisive factor in Park's favour. However, Jack Rowell, who had quit playing because of injury and stepped into the role of Gosforth's first coach, showed he was quickly mastering the art of preparing a side for the big day – Gosforth showed no fear and were certainly not in awe of the London side.

Rosslyn Park had flanker Bob Mordell sent off by referee Norman Sanson after only seven minutes for punching but Gosforth had already scored through Brian Patrick after a blindside run by Kenny Britton. The loss of Colin White with injury after twenty-one minutes to be replaced by Phil Levinson unsettled Gosforth and Park scored tries through Andy Ripley and Mike Bulpitt. A penalty from Weston and a drop goal from Ralston made it 14-9 in their favour but in the second half Terry Roberts scored a try, which was converted by Malcolm Young, and Steve Gustard blasted through for his 42nd try of the season to level the scores at 14-14. A late try by David Robinson was converted by Malcolm Young, who also kicked a penalty to bring the cup to Tyneside for the first time.

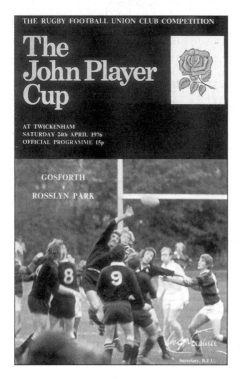

This is the front cover of the programme for the 1976 John Player Cup final, which was staged at Twickenham. It is an early example of programme design.

Gosforth second row John Short is just beaten to the ball in the John Player Cup final against Rosslyn Park at Twickenham.

The Gosforth side which won the 1976 John Player Cup final by 23-14 against Rosslyn Park at Twickenham. The club also retained the Northumberland Cup and won the Journal Trophy. From left to right, back row: J. Smith (president), D. Robinson, P. Levinson, I. Richardson, R. Breakey, T. Roberts, J. Rowell (coach), J. Short, A. Cutter, C. White, K. Britton, R. Wood (chairman of selectors). Middle row: P. Dixon, H. Patrick, S. Gustard, R. Uttley (captain), M. Young (vice-captain), B. Patrick, D. Madsen. Front row: R. Biggs, M. Griffin, D. Crawford, R. Mahoney. Not in picture: A. Preston.

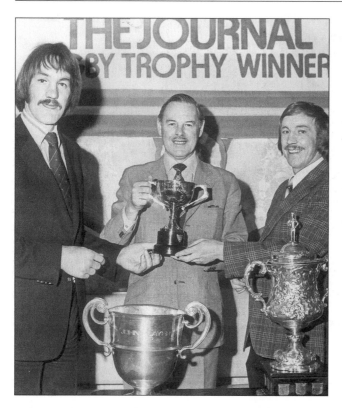

Gosforth celebrated their 1976 triple triumph at a special night in the North Road clubhouse when Len Harton, the managing director of the Newcastle Journal, *presented them with the* Journal Trophy. *The John Player Cup and the Northumberland County Cup are also on show as Roger Uttley (left) and Malcolm Young receive the Journal Trophy as the North-East's top club.*

It was, in fact, the first time a cup had been awarded to the winners as the RFU had signed a three-year sponsorship deal with John Player. The teams in that final were as follows:

Gosforth: B. Patrick, S.M. Griffin, J.K. Britton, H.E. Patrick, J.S. Gustard, R.W. Breakey, M. Young (captain), A.J. Cutter, D.F. Madsen, C. White (P. Levinson 21), T.C. Roberts, J.O. Short, A.J. Preston, D. Robinson, P.J. Dixon.

Rosslyn Park: P.A. Treseder (L. Byrne 33), M. Bulpitt, C.P. Kent, S. Fluskey, J.L. Moyes, C.S. Ralston, L.E. Weston, N.P. Hinton, P. d'A. Keith-Roach (captain), G. Lloyd-Roberts, A.K. Rodgers, N.D. Mantell, R. Mordell, D. Starling, A.G. Ripley.

The referee was N.R. Sanson of Berkshire.

On their way to the final Gosforth had beaten Hartlepool Rovers (35-9), Liverpool (19-12), Roundhay (14-3) and Sale (12-3) while Rosslyn Park had beaten Marlow (41-3), Penryn (39-3), Bristol (16-12) and Wakefield (12-6).

The following season Gosforth were back at Twickenham in what was probably the finest season in the club's history until the 1997 Premiership triumph. Fittingly, it was the club's centenary year and it was a huge success on and off the field. Besides retaining the John Player Cup by beating Waterloo 27-11, Gosforth won the Sunday Telegraph Pennant, topped the first RFU Northern Merit Table with a 100 per cent record, retained the Northumberland County Cup and the Journal Trophy and reached the finals of the

The 1976/77 season was one of the best in Gosforth's history as they retained the John Player Cup, Northumberland Senior Cup, Northern Merit Table, Sunday Telegraph Pennant, Journal Trophy and were runners-up in the Middlesex Sevens. The squad for the season was, from left to right, back row: R. Breakey, K. Britton, P. Dixon (inset), I. Richardson, A. Moor, J. Short, D. Percy, S. Archer, J. Hedley (inset), R. Mahoney, D.F. Madsen. Middle row: M. Mahoney (coach), C. White, D. Parker, T. Roberts, C. Blackett, P. Levinson, A. Cutter, R. Wood (chairman of selectors), J. Hutchison (chairman of playing). Front row: B.J.G. de Zwaan (president), S. Gustard, D. Robinson, R. Uttley (captain), M. Young (vice-captain), H. Patrick, B. Patrick.

prestigious Middlesex Sevens just a week after winning the John Player Cup. The club also supplied nineteen players to county rugby, three of them as captains – David Robinson (Cumbria), Colin White (Northumberland) and John Hedley (Durham). Through their success in retaining the John Player Cup and winning the first Northern Merit Table, Gosforth could rightly claim to be the best side in England, although Waterloo could dispute that. They won the unofficial Anglo-Welsh merit table and beat Gosforth in a non-merit table match at Blundellsands. However, Gosforth effectively settled the argument by beating Waterloo at Twickenham. Having missed the previous year's final with injury, Roger Uttley led the Gosforth side to their second success.

It wasn't an easy path to the final, although Gosforth enjoyed the advantage of being drawn at home in the first three rounds. They had to dispose of Coventry – still a formidable side – in the first round and it was close before Gosforth came through 12-6. Gosforth then crushed Fullerians 48-0 in the second round but the quarter-finals was a real tester, at home to Gloucester. It was not a pleasant match and had referee Norman Sanson seen what Mike Burton, the England prop, did in the final quarter of the game, he would certainly have sent him off. Sanson did not see the incident but George Burrell, the British Lions manager, who was in the crowd, did see it and the incident undoubtedly cost Burton a place in the Lions tour party to Australia. Gloucester had two tries disallowed and there were several flare-ups, but a solitary Malcolm Young penalty goal decided the match. As referee Norman Sanson left the pitch, he was barracked by disgruntled Gloucester fans and he needed the protection of some of the players on the way back to the dressing room.

The semi-finals saw Gosforth travel to London Welsh, who, while not the side they had been in the early 1970s, were going well that season after acquiring Bedford's cup-winning half-backs Neil Bennett and Alan Lewis. Bennett, despite his Welsh name, was an England international and could kick goals from anywhere as he had proved in the quarter-finals when he landed one from 60 metres to secure a 10-10 draw at Moseley and send his side through on the away team rule. Bennett kicked four penalties in the semi-final but Gosforth triumphed 18-12 and had not conceded a try on the way to the final.

They were clear favourites to retain the cup against Waterloo, who had finished second to them in the Northern Merit Table. A late injury scare involving Roger Uttley did not affect Gosforth's build-up to the final and they looked very assured, although there was an early shock within minutes of the start when Uttley departed with a torn ear. However, he returned after having the injury stitched and with his head swathed in bandages. He was back on the field only seconds before he saw Gosforth's proud record of not conceding a try in the competition disappear when Steve Christopherson scored. Nevertheless, Gosforth's pack assumed control and the team scored tries from Stewart Archer and Peter Dixon followed by two in two minutes from Dave Robinson. Brian

Gosforth captain Roger Uttley in action against London Welsh in the 1977 John Player Cup semi-final win.

John Hedley wins a crucial line-out for Gosforth in their second John Player Cup triumph against Waterloo at Twickenham in 1977.

Patrick kicked two conversions and a penalty as Gosforth won comfortably 27-14 after Steve Tickle had scored another try for Waterloo and Ian Ball kicked a penalty. The teams in the final were as follows:

Gosforth: B. Patrick, S. Archer, K. Britton, H. Patrick, S. Gustard, R. Breakey, M. Young, A. Cutter, D. Madsen, C. White, T. Roberts, J. Hedley, D. Robinson, P. Dixon, R. Uttley (captain).

Waterloo: S. Tickle, N. Spaven, G. Jackson, S. Christopherson, M. Flett, I. Ball, D. Carfoot, F. Blackhurst, C. Fisher (captain), D. Reed, M. Billingham, K. Short, K. Lunt, K. Hancock, L. Connor.

The referee was P. Hughes from Manchester.

Unfortunately, the victory over Waterloo was to be the club's last success at Twickenham until they won the Sanyo Cup twenty years later against the Rest of the World XV, although they would be beaten finalists in the 1981 John Player Cup and in 1998 they lost to Wasps in the Tetley's Bitter Cup final.

The exceptional 1976/77 season saw Gosforth lose just 2 and draw 1 of their 35 games, scoring 943 points and conceding just 179 in the process. Off the field, the club's centenary year highlight was a dinner in the Newcastle Civic Centre. The club also raised £20,000 – a lot of money in those days – to go on simultaneous tours to Boston and Italy.

Gosforth celebrated their centenary in 1977/78 by producing a souvenir brochure, which carried a specially designed centenary badge, as did their centenary dinner menu.

The Gosforth club were always great tourists and travellers, something which has continued with the Falcons. Their first tour was a 1953 trip to Denmark and on that tour was Mike Pearey, later to become president of the RFU. Trips to Cognac in France followed and the team also played in a four-cornered tournament in Boston, USA, as the representatives of the City of Newcastle, which was celebrating its 900th anniversary (it was Boston's 200th anniversary, hence the invitation).

The only misfortune in the 1976/77 season was that Roger Uttley missed touring New Zealand with the British Lions when a back injury on the eve of departure cost him his place. Earlier in the season, Uttley had captained an England side containing Malcolm Young and Peter Dixon to a 26-6 win over Scotland, who had Duncan Madsen at hooker. In that England *v*. Scotland match, both Malcolm Young and Roger Uttley scored tries and it was the first time that Gosforth had four players appearing in a Five Nations Championship match together. It was something that would not occur again for the club until the 1990s and little did anyone realize that victory over Waterloo was to be the club's last success at Twickenham until they won the Sanyo Cup twenty years later. They would, however, be beaten finalists in the 1981 John Player Cup and lose to Wasps in the 1998 Tetleys Bitter Cup final.

Gosforth were denied a hat-trick of Twickenham appearances the season following their second triumph when they lost to Gloucester, the eventual winners, in the second round at Kingsholm 19-10. It was a discgraceful match, with some of the Gloucester crowd spitting on the Gosforth players as they walked around the pitch before kick off. The game itself was punctuated by violence and it was not a great advert for the game. However, the season was

Malcolm Young breaks from the scrum during the battle at Kingsholm in 1978 when Gosforth lost 19-10 in the John Player Cup.

still a success as the Northumberland Cup was retained and second place to Liverpool in the Northern Merit Table was secured. Malcolm Young and Peter Dixon played for England, and Duncan Madsen and Richard Breakey for Scotland in the Five Nations Championship. In addition, John Butler and Colin White appeared for England 'B' against Romania and Jeff Bell for England Under-23s. Roger Uttley missed out again because of the back problems that plagued his career. The touring US Eagles also played at Gosforth losing 18-12, with Steve Gustard, Terry Roberts and Stewart Archer (the father of Garath) scoring tries and Mal Young kicking two penalties.

Gosforth never quite regained the dominance of the 1976/77 season. Gloucester's narrow 6-3 win over Leicester in the 1978 final signalled the start of the Tigers' John Player Cup reign, although Gosforth were to go so very close to gaining a third cup win over the next few seasons. They lost 6-3 at home to Moseley in the 1978/79 semi-finals – the first time any side had won in the Cup at Gosforth. Ironically, it was a pushover try that sealed Moseley's win against what was the best pack in England at the time – Gifford scored the try in the last few minutes and Akenhead converted. Furious Gosforth coach Mike Mahoney – his volcanic temper was legendary and his nickname of 'Grizzly' was well deserved – lambasted his side afterwards and also gave plenty of verbal responses to the unfortunate reporter who had the temerity to ask for a reaction, although it was from quite a safe distance!

The 1978/79 season was hardly vintage stuff but Gosforth lost only 4 and drew 1 of their 33 games under captain Peter Dixon. On an individual level, centre Alan MacMillan toured with England to the Far East. In addition, John Butler played for the Barbarians and the

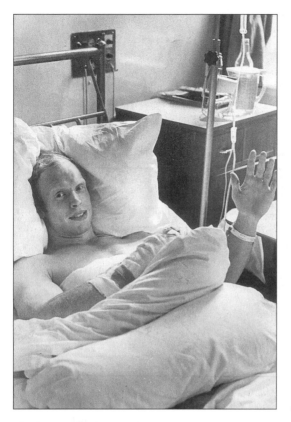

Gosforth prop Colin White puts a brave face on things after a horrific chainsaw accident in 1978 in which he lost some fingers from his right hand. White made an amazing comeback to play and captain Gosforth and also appear for England.

Terry Roberts gets the ball away during the 1979 John Player Cup semi-final against Moseley which Gosforth lost 6-3.

Gosforth club president Ray Wood receives a special cartoon by Dudley Hallwood from Len Harton, managing director of the Newcastle Chronicle and Journal *to mark the opening of the club's new President's Room.*

North against the All Blacks along with Mal Young, Peter Dixon and Jeff Bell while Uttley, Dixon and Young also played for England against the New Zealanders.

Gosforth had slipped to fifth in the Northern Merit Table and would have missed out on the following season's John Player Cup as only the top four went forward. However, champions Liverpool also qualified as Lancashire Cup winners and that meant Gosforth took their Merit Table spot as the fifth-placed team. This was a fortunate if bizarre way to qualify for the 1979/80 competition, but the team looked like making it really count before their luck again turned sour with a third round defeat at Harlequins. Gosforth were drawing 3-3 with five minutes left and heading for the semi-finals on the away team rule, but a wicked bounce deceived both Richard Breakey and Brian Patrick, allowing Quins to score and convert for a 9-3 win. In the previous round Gosforth had given one of their best ever cup performances in winning 14-3 at Bristol after a narrow 10-6 first round win at Hartlepool Rovers. Leicester, the winners the previous season 15-12 against Moseley, retained the cup 21-9 against London Irish.

Captained by Colin White, Gosforth finished fifth again in the Northern Merit Table in 1979/80 when they lost 9 of their 38 games. However, they qualified for the following season's John Player Cup again because Roundhay won the Yorkshire Cup as well as finishing fourth in the table behind Orrell, Fylde and West Hartlepool.

There was a worrying indication that Gosforth were not producing real quality players when, for the first time in many years, the club had no one appearing in the Five Nations Championship, although John Butler did gain an England trial and played for England 'B' alongside Colin White.

35

4

DECLINE AND FALL

The 1980s were to prove a difficult time for Gosforth though, on the face of it, they had every reason to be optimistic about the their prospects. However, there was a real body blow when England's Roger Uttley departed to London to take up a post at Harrow School. Uttley joined Wasps and his departure hastened the break-up of the great Gosforth side of the 1970s. Players such as Kenny Britton, Peter Dixon, Dave Robinson, Duncan Madsen, John Hedley and Steve Gustard were all about to or had already retired, although there were still good players coming through the ranks to wear the green and white hoops, particularly from the club's Cumbrian connection (thanks to Robinson). The likes of Neil 'Maxi' McDowell, Paul Cusack, Mike Lowther and big No. 8 Mark Richardson were all talented players, although injury and approaches from other clubs – including Rugby League in the case of the Cumbrians – was always a threat.

Paul Simpson, a very talented back row forward, was a good example of the problems Gosforth had in hanging on to their players. He quickly established himself in the Gosforth back row where he proved to be a real game-breaker with his ability to score tries. However, he was lured away by Bath and although he did play for England, he never really fulfilled his potential. Much the same could be said of Simon Edwards, another powerful back row forward who could score tries at will, but serious knee injuries eventually put paid to his career at the top level.

With players like Steve Bainbridge, Stewart Archer, David 'Banty' Johnson (who was to rival Malcolm Young in the club point-scoring records), Simon Smith and Bob Anderson coming through as well as the Cumbrian connection, Gosforth were still very much top dogs in the North. They could also more than hold their own nationally, as they were to prove in the 1980/81 season when that campaign gave them genuine reason to believe they were back in business as one of the country's leading clubs. The team won 34 and drew 1 of their 40 games and Malcolm Young led the try-scoring stakes with 15 of the 117 scored. A very productive cup run saw Gosforth return to Twickenham for their third John Player Cup final.

There were signs that the younger players were becoming fixtures in the side. David Johnson, who was starting to take over the kicking role from Young (when he was able to get his hands on the ball first), landed 184 points and was making a name for himself with drop goals after slotting 10 during the season. Richard Breakey had switched from fly-half to centre to make room for David Johnson and there was an argument whether this was the best move for the side. Nevertheless, with Johnson's uncanny ability to hoof the ball a long way for a player of no great physical stature, Malcolm Young's equally devastating left boot, Breakey's priceless ability to step off either foot and accelerate in tight situations and Stewart Archer's powerhouse wing play, Gosforth were a pretty good all-round side. The team were certainly forward orientated (as they had been in the mid-1970s) and this did not endear them to the national press. This mattered little to Gosforth as they won the Northumberland Cup again

Alan MacMillan, who came close to winning a full cap for England, cuts back inside in a match against Wilmslow during the 1979/80 season.

and, more importantly, the Northern Merit Table with a 100 per cent record to ensure continued John Player Cup qualification – still the real measure of a club's success in the absence of a properly structured league system.

The highlight of the season was undoubtedly reaching the John Player Cup final, although there was to be disappointment at Twickenham for the first time. With the new wider system of qualification involving county cup winners and merit tables, Gosforth had byes through the first two rounds. In the third round they had a fairly comfortable passage, winning 17-7 at home to Fylde, but it was a real battle at Waterloo in the fourth round after some ill-advised comments from Gosforth players about how easy it would be appeared in the press and served as maximum motivation for the Merseysiders, who ran Gosforth close before going down 12-9. Away at Nottingham in the quarter-finals did not prove as difficult a task and Gosforth cruised through 23-3. This was Nottingham's heaviest home defeat for sixteen months and it brought Moseley back to the New Ground for the semi-finals. There was to be no repeat of 1979 as Malcolm Young, Alan MacMillan and Richard Breakey tore Moseley apart in a 24-3 win – Moseley's heaviest cup defeat in a decade.

The final turned out to be one of the best ever seen at Twickenham. With their big pack and powerful backs, Gosforth were clear favourites to be the first club to win the John Player Cup three times and get to keep the trophy, but it did not turn out that way. The Leicester fans were silenced shortly after kick off when the Gosforth forwards nonchalantly rolled the Tigers pack back some thirty metres from their own ten-metre line deep into the Leicester half. It seemed only a matter of time with Steve Bainbridge, who was soon to play for England and the British Lions, dominating the line-outs, but the Leicester pack refused to lie down and their tackling behind the scrum nullified Gosforth's back row.

At half-time the score was 12-6 with referee Roger Quittenton (London and Sussex), whose quixotic officiating had always been a mystery to Gosforth, deciding to award a string of penalties in Leicester's favour. Dusty Hare kicked two and converted a try by Steve Kenney while David Johnson kicked two penalties for Gosforth. Brian Patrick's massive fifty-metre penalty goal made it 12-9 and in a fizzing second half there was plenty of controversy. Quittenton allowed Leicester to take a quick throw-in when it wasn't their ball (much to Malcolm Young's fury), a fight erupted in midfield and when it all subsided the Leicester backs, who had wisely decided not to get involved in the punch-up, had swept the ball wide with Barnwell scoring in the corner. The match was all but over when Hare scored a converted try by chipping and chasing. Young sent Anderson and Butler down the short side for Rob Cunningham's consolation try, which was converted by Johnson to make it 22-15.

The teams for the final were as follows:

Gosforth: B. Patrick, J.S. Archer, R.W. Breakey, A.J. MacMillan, N.H. McDowell, D. Johnson, M. Young, J.A.H. Bell, R. Cunningham, C. White (captain), T. Roberts, S. Bainbridge, S.M. Smith, T.R. Anderson, J.L. Butler.

Leicester: W.H. Hare, K. Williams, P.W. Dodge, C.R. Woodward, R.C. Barnwell, L. Cusworth, S. Kenney, S. Redfern, P. Wheeler (captain), R.J. Cowling, N. Joyce, J. Jackson, S.R. Johnson (A.P. Collington 82), I. Smith, G.J. Adey.

Leicester had beaten Roundhay, Bristol, Sale and London Scottish in the previous rounds.

It was also a very successful season for the North-East region as Northumberland, with thirteen Gosforth players in the side, won the County Championship in their centenary year, beating Gloucestershire at Kingsholm.

Although Gosforth's loss at Twickenham took a lot of the shine off the year, there were still plenty of individual triumphs. Both Steve Bainbridge and Jeff Bell played for England 'B', Rob

John Butler wins another line-out. The Cumbrian lock was a mainstay of the Gosforth side in the 1980s and many believe he should have played for England.

The programme from the 1981 John Player Cup final when Gosforth and Leicester were both going for a hat-trick of wins. It wasn't Gosforth's day, however, and the Tigers took permanent possession of the original John Player Cup.

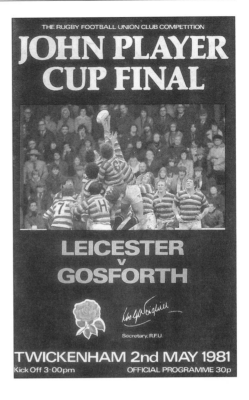

THE RUGBY FOOTBALL UNION CLUB COMPETITION

JOHN PLAYER CUP FINAL

LEICESTER
v
GOSFORTH

Secretary, R.F.U.

TWICKENHAM 2nd MAY 1981
Kick Off 3·00pm   OFFICIAL PROGRAMME 30p

Cunningham appeared for Scotland 'B', Bainbridge and Brian Patrick went on tour to Argentina with England during the summer, Richard Breakey went to New Zealand with Scotland and Neil McDowell played for England Under-23.

After such a successful season Gosforth must have had few fears for their future, but within a relatively short space of time and certainly by the end of the 1980s the club was in the throes of a serious decline. Another real setback was the departure of coach Mike Mahoney, who had taken over from Jack Rowell in 1977. Mahoney left to take up a new job – a perennial problem for Gosforth with many players and officials seeking their fortune elsewhere, often in London.

Mahoney is the first to admit that he might not have been the most politic of men and he also had a temper that was legendary. However, no one could fault his commitment and passion for the Gosforth club. He coached them in three spells: twice in the 1980s and once in the 1990s, when they achieved First Division league status for the first time (albeit briefly).

Mahoney's departure after the 1980/81 season saw Dave Robinson take over as coach. The following season, Peter Scurfield, a former Gosforth, Alnwick and Liverpool player, assumed the reins. Mahoney returned in 1985, only for work demands to again take him out of the area in 1987 when he was succeeded by former club and county captain Steve Gustard.

Mahoney's third spell was as the club's first Director of Rugby in 1990 when Gosforth became Newcastle Gosforth. Although he took them into the first division in 1992/93, it was a short-lived stay – both for the club in the first division and for Mahoney in charge. Relegation the following season led to the sack – a decision that was both short-sighted and extremely damaging in the long-term as it ushered in one of the most difficult periods in the club's history.

Coach Steve Gustard was placed in temporary charge following Mahoney's departure and Alan Old, the former England and Middlesbrough player, was eventually brought in as Director of Coaching but his tenure was brief. He lasted just under twelve months before he became the victim of player power. A delegation of senior players met with the club's board of management and, with Gosforth languishing at the foot of Division Two and threatened by relegation, Old was asked to resign. Harry Patrick, another former captain, was installed as caretaker coach and then appointed club coach. His period in charge was equally brief because by the end of September 1995, Newcastle Gosforth as it had become, was taken over by Sir John Hall's Newcastle Sporting Club as the sport heralded the arrival of professionalism.

There were no signs of the traumatic events that lay ahead, as the season that followed the 1980/81 John Player Cup final appearance was another successful one. Although their nemesis Leicester knocked them out of the John Player Cup at the quarter-final stage, Gosforth finished second in the Northern Merit Table to Wakefield, retained the Northumberland Cup and Journal Trophy and won 31 of their 35 games, scoring 924 points and conceding just 289. Steve Bainbridge was capped for England and, along with Neil McDowell, toured the USA and Canada with England during the summer.

Brian Patrick was skipper for the 1982/83 season, but the team was nowhere near as successful as the previous two years. The club's record was 27 wins, 12 losses and 3 draws from their 42 games, but they slipped to third in the Northern Merit Table behind Sale and Orrell. Heavy defeats by Gala and Hawick at the start of the season set a pattern and injury problems meant that David Johnson missed half the season – at one stage Malcolm Young had to be called out of retirement. At the end of the season John Butler and Richard Breakey also decided

Still leaving them on their backsides into the 1980s. Mal Young is supported by John Hedley in a match against Wilmslow.

Gosforth missed out on the John Player Cup the previous season after losing to Leicester in the final, but they were still a formidable outfit as the 1981/82 line-up shows. From left to right, back row: P. Scurfield (coach), J. Bell, C. White, T. Roberts, S. Lewis, J. Storey, J. Gray, B. Jennings, J. Butler, S. Bainbridge, J. Blissett, P. Simpson, T. Hogg. Middle row: S. Byrne, N. McDowell, S. Gustard, R. Anderson (captain), M. Young, D. Johnson, B. Patrick. Front row: J. Chappell, D. Briggs, H. Patrick, J. Pollock.

to retire, but there were still signs that quality players were joining the club. These included Scotland wing Jim Pollock and back row Simon Edwards, who were joint top try scorers with 13, while Steve Bainbridge became a British Lion and prop Jon Curry played for England Under-23s in Romania.

There was some improvement in the 1983/84 season, which saw Bob Anderson as captain, although there was a shock when Alnwick prevented a fourteenth consecutive win in the Northumberland Cup. Wasps also knocked them out of the John Player Cup in the third round with a 12-12 draw – the London club going through by scoring more tries. The record of 29 wins and 3 draws from 43 games was not what the North Road Ground club were used to, although there were plenty of celebrations when Colin White was capped for England at long last and Steve Bainbridge retained his place in the second row. Jim Pollock also played on the wing for Scotland.

David Johnson, who was fit again, scored 334 points and his prolific return masked the growing problems that Gosforth were having in matching the top national sides and the growing challenge of West Hartlepool as an alternative for the region's top players. West finished top of the Northern Merit Table and Gosforth had to be content with fourth place behind Sale and Waterloo.

The club's decline gathered pace in 1984/85 with Steve Bainbridge moving to Fylde to take up a new job, captain Steve Gustard retiring and both Brian Patrick and Neil McDowell leaving the club. Top try scorer Simon Edwards' career was blighted by knee injuries, which were to force him into retirement from top class rugby. David Johnson still managed to score 362 points and Jim Pollock 17 tries, although 14 defeats was the most that Gosforth had conceded for many years. The Northumberland Cup was regained but Gosforth slipped to

Gosforth full-back Brian Patrick, possibly the best uncapped full-back in England during the 1980s, clears his lines against Wakefield.

Gosforth played host to several touring sides during the 1980s including Zimbabwe. Here, club president Ken Lockerbie (right) greets Col. Robin Brown, vice-president of the Zimbabwe RFU, with Ray Wood in the centre.

Ray Wood, former Gosforth president and chairman of selectors, is installed as president of Northumberland in 1984 by Dennis Douglas, the previous year's president.

sixth in the Northern Merit Table and went out of the John Player Cup at the third round stage again, losing 16-13 to a Saracens late penalty at Southgate.

In 1985/86 there was a national merit table system for the first time, which consisted of two tables. However, it was hardly satisfactory as not every club played each other. Although Gosforth were included in Division A, they promptly lost that status the following season. This was the team's first experience of relegation and that cast a pall over the campaign although they lost only 8 and drew 1 of their 36 matches.

There was some consolation in finishing runners-up to Waterloo in the Northern Merit Table, which was still running despite the national merit tables. There was more disappointment, however, in losing in the John Player Cup on the away team rule after holding Northampton to a third round 6-6 draw at the North Road Ground. It was the second time in three seasons that the club had suffered this fate and a competition that had proved so lucky for Gosforth in the 1970s had certainly turned sour in the 1980s. Once again, it was a season beset with injuries and more than fifty players were used, including Malcolm Young, who was called out of retirement again to cover a crisis at scrum-half.

Jon Curry captained a young Gosforth side to 25 wins out of 41 matches in 1986/87 and players such as David Ogilvie, Simon Smith and Dave 'Dozy' Davidson played for the Anglo-Scots. Although Gosforth discovered a real talent in Richard Petyt, a student at Newcastle University, they still finished fifth from bottom of the John Smiths National Merit Table B. This was viewed as a disappointment, as was losing to Leicester 19-6 in the fourth round of the John Player Cup after a narrow 10-9 win over Waterloo in the third round.

Gosforth could hardly have chosen a worse time to be on the slide, with the advent of a nationwide league system headed by three national divisions. On their recent performances it was hardly surprising that they were placed in Division Two when the Courage League was launched in the 1987/88 season. Frankly, Gosforth were lucky to avoid relegation to the third division after winning just 3 and drawing 1 of their 11 league games – and one of those wins was deleted after it was embarrassingly discovered that they had inadvertently fielded an

Two of Gosforth's most influential captains in the 1980s – Bob Anderson (left) and Steve Gustard – played the game in uncompromising style; Anderson at flanker and Gustard on the wing.

ineligible player. This put them on 17 points and level with Blackheath, whom they shaded on points difference as Northampton, with 13 points, were relegated. There was also a 33-9 hammering at home by Moseley in the John Player Cup and a total of 15 games were lost. Moreover, signs of financial instability were beginning to surface. These were to plague the club throughout the late 1980s and early 1990s, and would eventually lead to the sale of the North Road Ground and a move to Kingston Park.

It was also around this time that David Campbell advocated using Gosforth as the basis for the formation of a Newcastle area side. Campbell had played for Gosforth in the second row and back row in the 1960s and 1970s, and was to play a vital role in the takeover of the club by Sir John Hall's Sporting Club in 1995. He made a concerted attempt to persuade the North-East clubs to support the idea and a series of open meetings involving local clubs were initially encouraging and showed promise. However, the proposal never got to any formal stage, with the idea foundering on the understandable parochialism of the clubs and also the understandable resentment many of them felt towards Gosforth, whom they believed had poached their best players throughout the 1970s and 1980s.

Relegation was only just avoided again in the 1988/89 season with Gosforth finishing one point ahead of London Scottish and London Welsh, who went down. There was some improvement with 4 wins out of 11 league games but Gosforth, with Giles Smallwood as captain, came close to losing as many games as they won with a record of played 40, won 21, drawn 1, lost 18. They scored 732 points and conceded 652. In addition, there was now the customary and depressing early defeat in the John Player Cup, this time 29-9 at home to Wakefield in the third round.

5
NEW GROUND AGAIN

If Gosforth's luck had generally been poor for most of the 1980s, it certainly took a turn for the better in the 1989/90 season though they had perhaps their worst season for results since they became a senior club. They won just 1 and drew 1 of their 11 Division Two games and they lost 22 and drew 1 of their 40 games during the season. The team finished bottom of Courage Division Two and would have been relegated but for league reorganisation, which saw the size of the national leagues increased. Just how lucky Gosforth were in this respect is probably appreciated more now than then. Going down into Division Three would have been disastrous and a setback which may have proved fatal for the long-term future of top-class rugby in Newcastle.

There were mitigating circumstances for Gosforth's appalling record in the 1989/90 season. They had sold their North Road Ground and were in the process of moving to Kingston Park but, as their new ground wasn't going be ready until the following season, they decided to play all their home games at Percy Park's ground in North Shields. Not for the first time in the club's history, Gosforth were effectively homeless, though they did have the prospect of somewhere to go this time.

Newcastle Gosforth said goodbye to the New Ground when they took the plunge and sold their clubhouse and pitches as they moved into the 1990s.

The speed at which they sold their North Road Ground to house builders Cussins for £1.76m and bought the *Newcastle Chronicle and Journal* sports ground at Kingston Park, near Kenton Bank Foot, for a bargain £55,000 was astonishing.

The sum of £60,000 – of which around £5,000 was spent on buying some additional land – may have been a lot of money in the late 1980s but it really was a steal. The only drawback was that Gosforth had to spend a very large chunk of what they made from the sale of the North Road Ground on a new clubhouse, stand and three new pitches. Nevertheless, they took the plunge, basing their hopes on the premise they could make their clubhouse pay its way and finance the club by hiring out the building and making sure the turnover was at the top end of the scale. This was wishful thinking.

While planning permission for the Kingston Park ground and clubhouse was being sought and building started, Gosforth played their home league games at Percy Park, although they did take their fourth round John Player Cup-tie against Gloucester to Gateshead's International Stadium. They lost 26-15, but it was not a performance to be ashamed of.

The sale of the North Road Ground, the purchase of Kingston Park and the building of the new clubhouse was masterminded by Ken Lockerbie, who also later stepped in as chairman of the board of management to steer the club through some choppy waters in the 1990s. It is fair to say that Newcastle Falcons are now the proud owners of a magnificent playing surface and a ground with enormous potential thanks to Lockerbie's efforts and those of several other club officials including John Gray. He was club president for three years at three different grounds – at the North Road (1988/89), Percy Park (1989/90) and Kingston Park (1990/91) – and went on to become Northumberland County president in 1996/97. Gray was still very much involved with the club as a director of Newcastle Falcons and a

Mike Mahoney, Newcastle Gosforth's first Director of Rugby, is happy as the new Kingston Park clubhouse and pitch takes shape.

The Kingston Park stand and clubhouse soon after opening. It is now facing further redevelopment.

An aerial view of Kingston Park without the temporary stands which go up at the start of each new season.

member of the Newcastle Gosforth Shareholders Association board of management following the acquisition of the club by David Thompson from Sir John Hall's Sporting Club in 1999.

Moving to Kingston Park was not a foregone conclusion. There were discussions with neighbours Northern about a possible merger or ground sharing and the idea was suggested that Northern should sell McCracken Park and both clubs move into Kingston Park together. Similar discussions took place at various times throughout the 1980s and 1990s, often varying in intensity depending on relations between the two clubs. This often depended on how much hostility there had been in the annual Boxing Day derby! While there seemed to be agreement on at least two occasions, one or other always shied away from the final commitment. It would not have been a marriage made in heaven that's for sure.

Newcastle Gosforth were in their new home for the start of the 1990/91 season – the decision to add Newcastle to the name Gosforth had been taken at the club's annual meeting. An RFU President's XV including Will Carling, Rory Underwood, Dean Richards, Paul Ackford, Jeff Probyn, Richard Hill, Chris Oti and a certain Rob Andrew played at Kingston Park to officially open the new ground. The late Mike Pearey, a former Gosforth player and president of the RFU, also officially opened the clubhouse.

Newcastle Gosforth lost the match 32-6 in front of a crowd of 3,000 and the teams that day, 8 September 1990, were as follows:

Newcastle Gosforth: J. Whisker, G. Spearman, P. Holdstock, C. Leslie (R. Wilkinson 40), M. Winham, P. Clark, S. Douglas, I. Davies (I. Shanks 44), N. Frankland, M. Fraser, K. Westgarth, T. Roberts (captain), B. Chick, J. Baldwin, S. Bainbridge.

RFU Presidents XV: A. Buzza (Wasps), R. Underwood (Leicester), W. Carling (Harlequins, captain), J. Buckton (Saracens), C. Oti (Wasps), R. Andrew (Wasps), R. Hill (Bath), J. Leonard (Harlequins), J. Olver (Northampton), J. Probyn (Wasps), S. Shortland (Northampton), P. Ackford (Harlequins), M. Teague (Gloucester), P. Winterbottom (Harlequins), D. Richards (Leicester).

The match was refereed by D. Leslie from Scotland. Paul Ackford, Rory Underwood, Alan Buzza, Dean Richards and Chris Oti (two) scored tries for England, Rob Andrew converted one and Graeme Spearman kicked two penalties for Newcastle Gosforth.

It turned out to be a fairly successful first season at Kingston Park. Terry Roberts led the club to 24 wins out of 34 and sixth place in Courage Division Two, although there was defeat in the fourth round of the Pilkington Cup (formerly the John Player Cup) at home to Orrell by 26-9.

Mike Mahoney, installed the previous season as the club's first paid Director of Rugby in charge of coaching, was back doing what he liked best – turning the Green and Whites into a formidable force. One of his best moves around this time was to bring over three New Zealand players. One didn't last too long and disappeared after a season, the second, Mark Beattie, was to play with some success in the centre for Newcastle Gosforth before moving on to Blaydon while the third, Richard Arnold, turned out to be one the best signings any club has ever made.

Mahoney met up with the Kiwi trio at Newcastle airport and initially could not believe that Arnold was a second row because he was clearly not big enough to play there. He was all set to offload Arnold but after one training session Mahoney knew he had a quality back row forward, not a second row, on his hands. Arnold went on to captain the club and, like Arthur Smith, Ray McLoughlin, Roger Uttley and Dave Robinson before him, substantially changed the attitude of the players around him towards training, their approach to the game and commitment to their club. Not surprisingly, ten years on, Richard Arnold is still a valued member of the Newcastle Falcons squad and was awarded a testimonial year, the only Newcastle player so far to be granted such a reward.

Arnold must have wondered what he was letting himself in for when he arrived on Tyneside from Eltham, a small town on the west coast of the North Island of New Zealand. Arnold describes his home town as consisting of 'three pubs, a supermarket, a cheese factory, and 3,000 people'. He admits he came to England looking for a bit of fun, but he didn't bank on an armed siege and riots:

> We moved into a terraced house in Lemington. I'd only seen back-to-back
> houses on the credits of *Coronation Street* at home in New Zealand and thought

New Zealander Mark Beattie (left) and Richard Arnold shortly after they had been signed by Director of Rugby Mike Mahoney.

they didn't really exist. All of a sudden we were faced with row upon row of them and we were living in one of them. One day there was a knock on the door at two o'clock in the morning and when we opened it a load of coppers were standing outside. There was an armed siege next door – they had come to arrest a guy who had committed a murder in the city centre and told us to move into the room next door in case any bullets came through the wall! We'd been living next to this dangerous character for six months without realising it.

Then there were the riots in the west end of Newcastle – just down the road from us – which also took place during our year in Lemington. The telly was full of shots of burning buildings and overturned cars every night – right on our doorstep!

But things did get better, although when I arrived I was skint and worked in a Newcastle health club to make a few quid, for which I was very grateful.

I'd decided to take a year out and come to England. My brother Tony saw an advert in the magazine *Rugby World* stating that Newcastle Gosforth, as the club was known then, wanted players.

Mark Beattie and Arnold applied, even though Newcastle Gosforth were seeking big second rows, but after Mike Mahoney saw both in action, he changed his mind and, in the case of Arnold, a ten-year association with Newcastle had begun.

With John Curry as captain in 1991/92 and Arnold in the side, Newcastle Gosforth's

England and British Lions second row Steve Bainbridge in line-out action. Bainbridge continued to play for Gosforth and Newcastle Gosforth during the 1980s and 1990s before his job took him to Spain, where he played in the Spanish first division.

improvement continued. Fourth place in Courage Division Two and a narrow 10-0 defeat in a titanic quarter-final home Pilkington Cup-tie by Leicester showed they were very much on the up. However, West Hartlepool's promotion to Division One of the Courage League was a serious blow for Newcastle Gosforth's reputation as the North-East's top club and would make recruitment of players ever more difficult, given that they now had the alternative of top flight rugby at Brierton Lane just thirty miles down the road.

A possible merger with Northern was back on the agenda in 1992 when they approached Newcastle Gosforth with the offer of talks, following discussions Northern members had had about selling one of their pitches for housing to finance a clubhouse rebuilding scheme. The first talks with Northern had been in 1988/89 when Gosforth were negotiating the sale of their North Road Ground to various developers and builders but Northern pulled out after they won the Northumberland Cup, believing that heralded an upturn in their fortunes.

Once again, Northern pulled out of the talks after members voted against a merger or amalgamation in the February of 1992 and Northern pursued their plan to sell off one of their pitches and rebuild their clubhouse.

Newcastle Gosforth were also in talks with Northumberland County at around the same time with regard to a possible centre of excellence at Kingston Park and negotiations did proceed to a fairly advanced stage before foundering for a variety of reasons. These included internal bickering in both organisations, antagonism against Newcastle Gosforth and the reluctance of Northumberland to part with any of the money they had made from the sale of the County Ground.

It was perhaps fortunate that the merger talks with Northern did disappear from the agenda as it allowed Newcastle Gosforth to concentrate fully on winning promotion from Courage Division Two, which they achieved by winning 10 of their 12 league games in 1992/93. They were given a thorough hammering, though, in the fourth round of the Pilkington Cup, losing 33-3 to Northampton. This result should have rung some alarm bells, but promotion was the major prize and possibly convinced the club that they could make the step up without too much trouble.

Newcastle Gosforth passed West Hartlepool going in the opposite direction after the Brierton Lane club finished twelfth in their first season in Division One. There was no gloating over West Hartlepool's fate at Kingston Park, which is just as well because it was an experience that was to come their way the following season. For the moment, however, Newcastle Gosforth were able to revel in acquiring first division status in the Courage League for the first time.

Captained by Neil Frankland, the team was a mixture of experience and talented youngsters. Veteran second row Terry Roberts was still playing along with David Johnson at fly-half and Jon Curry at prop. The back line included players such as Ross Wilkinson, Steve Douglas and Ian Chandler with Richard Arnold and Martin Corry in the forwards. There was a real sense of achievement at Kingston Park and their first campaign in Courage Division One was viewed with optimism and anticipation.

This optimism was misplaced and Newcastle Gosforth found their assessment that the squad which had won them promotion to the top flight would be good enough to survive there was way off beam but, to be honest, there was precious little to recruit on their own doorstep. Even if there had been, the club didn't have the money or the infrastructure to offer

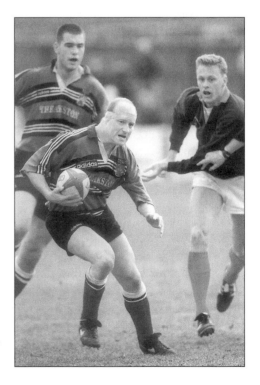

Neil Frankland captained Newcastle Gosforth in 1993/94 when they were briefly in the first division. His career with the club spanned fourteen years and he played with distinction at both hooker and flanker.

Director of Rugby Mick Mahoney at work with the Newcastle Gosforth forwards as they prepare for their first season in Courage Division One in 1993/94.

the jobs and cars the London, South-West and Midland clubs could.

A 42-12 defeat at Orrell was a rude awakening to Division One and, although their first home game in Division One at Kingston Park was a 12-12 draw with Gloucester, defeats at the hands of Wasps, Harlequins, Leicester and Bath, quickly established Newcastle Gosforth as the Division One chopping blocks. A fifth round exit to Orrell in the fifth round of the Pilkington Cup 12-7 only served to increase the pressure as Newcastle Gosforth slid towards relegation and by March 1994 the club were already doomed to a return to Division Two.

Relegation cost Mike Mahoney his job as Director of Rugby. Following a meeting with club chairman Geoff Brown, Mahoney resigned, although there is no doubt he was given little option but to go. Little thought seemed to have been given to lining up a successor and coach Steve Gustard was placed in temporary charge. Alan Old, the former Middlesbrough, Sheffield and England fly-half, was eventually appointed as the club's Director of Coaching (not Director of Rugby) but he eventually fared little better than Mahoney although the club finished third in Courage Division Two in 1994/95.

Old's appointment cost Newcastle Gosforth the services of Steve Gustard, who was told he was no longer required. It seemed a churlish decision and Gustard moved on to coach at Blaydon. The decision to oust Mahoney and then Gustard was to have serious repercussions as it stripped the club of two men who had shown themselves capable of recruiting new players. Nevertheless, there were promising players in the Newcastle Gosforth squad that season under the captaincy of Richard Arnold. These included future England players Martin Corry and Garath Archer as well as Richard Metcalfe, who was to go on to play for Scotland. Lock John Fowler and craggy prop Paul Van-Zandvliet, who would be a part of the Falcons championship-winning squad, were in the pack and among the backs were talented players Simon Mason, who was to play full-back for Ireland, David Casado, Tim Penn, Matt Tetlow

 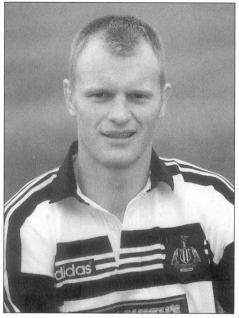

The changing face of Richard Arnold, the only Newcastle player to be granted a testimonial to date. Crew-cut and just off the plane from New Zealand (left) and still crew-cut but thinning a bit after ten years playing for Newcastle (right).

and experienced Scotland international Richard Cramb along with England 'A' scrum-half Steve Douglas and centres Ross Wilkinson and Ian Chandler.

There were wins that season against the likes of Fylde, Wakefield, Waterloo, Moseley and Nottingham but, against top-class opposition, Newcastle Gosforth struggled. This was shown most clearly when they were hammered 58-12 by Wasps in the fourth round of the Pilkington Cup. There were also ominous signs that the club's perennial problem of paying their way was becoming a very serious situation and there was a sense of frustration within the club that little seemed to be going their way. The financial situation was so bad that there were fears of the club having to close down, especially after it was announced there had been a lost of £30,000 on the year with an overdraft that was becoming unmanageable.

Geoff Brown resigned as chairman towards the end of 1994, with Ken Lockerbie stepping in to take over. Old's tenure as Director of Coaching ended after less than twelve months when he was shown the door in April 1995, after a delegation of six senior players met with Lockerbie and the board of management and left them in no doubt that they had lost confidence in the coach. The players claimed that there was no pattern or policy and the departure of the likes of John Fowler, Garath Archer, Martin Corry and Simon Mason would seem to back them up. Old resigned and Harry Patrick was appointed caretaker coach and then given the job full time. It was possibly the shortest appointment for a coach on record as one of the biggest shock waves to hit the game of rugby was about to explode.

6
BIRTH OF THE FALCONS

The International Board's decision to declare the game 'open' or professional on 26 August 1995 caught everyone by surprise. Pushed by the Southern Hemisphere countries, who had been paying their players for years, the return of South Africa to the rugby fold and the advent of the Tri-Nations and Super 10 tournaments (soon to become the Super 12), which was backed by television cash, the International Board, the last bastion of amateurism, simply caved in and allowed a free-for-all.

Most of the game's recent problems can be traced back to the decision to simply open up the game with no apparent planning or forethought. If the IB were slow to realise the implications, then the Home Unions of England, Scotland, Wales and Ireland were even slower on the uptake. This was to prove crucial in the first year of professionalism as it allowed the clubs to sign up the top players to contracts – unlike New Zealand, South Africa and Australia where the players were swiftly contracted to their national union.

All this seemed light years away from the problems Newcastle Gosforth were experiencing, but it was ultimately to prove their salvation. However, it needed a bold stroke of imagination from two Scots and one Englishman before Newcastle Gosforth would shake rugby to its foundations. A glut of resignations had led to David Campbell and Derek Balfour being elected to the Newcastle Gosforth board of management, with the former as Chairman of Rugby. Campbell was a long-time advocate of a Newcastle area side as the way forward for rugby in the North-East. He initially suggested the idea in the 1980s, held a series of open meetings with local clubs but failed to get a clear commitment as parochial self-interest dominated and the idea was shelved.

Merger talks between Gosforth and Northern and then Newcastle Gosforth and Northern had reawakened Campbell's interest and the former Gosforth second row urged both clubs not to miss the opportunity again. Nevertheless, when Northern dropped out of the talks a second time in 1992, the concept of an area side seemed dead and buried forever. However, Campbell was to see the birth of his dream of a Newcastle side – albeit in a different form to what he had expected. He had come back into club affairs as a member of the Newcastle Gosforth board of management but was already becoming disillusioned after being told the rugby budget for the 1995/96 season needed to be cut by some £50,000 because of the parlous state of the club's finances.

In fact, there was a very real threat that Newcastle Gosforth would not survive the season and if they went down to Division Three, which was the gloomy pre-season prediction, there was a real likelihood that the club would slide further down the Courage Leagues and become a rugby backwater – if they survived at all. West Hartlepool's escape from relegation the previous season also brought its problems for Newcastle Gosforth. They were able to offer Richard Metcalfe, Richard Arnold and

Scotland flanker Peter Walton first division rugby. All three left Kingston Park and headed to Brierton Lane for the 1995/96 season and Martin Corry moved to Bristol.

Ironically, the possibility of a merger with Northern had been back on the agenda at the end of the previous season, the idea being that Northern would sell McCracken Park to a developer (a figure of £5 million was said to be on the table) and move in with Newcastle Gosforth at Kingston Park. It was, of all things, a win in the Northumberland Cup final for Northern, when they defeated Tynedale 6-3, that convinced the McCracken Park club they were set for better times and strong enough to survive on their own. Yet again, Northern went cold on the idea of a merger.

The disappearance of any possible deal with Northern at the end of the 1994/95 season was no great cause for disappointment at Kingston Park, where the loss of players and the dire financial plight of the club as the 1995/96 season approached was of more concern. There was little expectation of a major sponsor bailing out the club and with a shrinking rugby budget, Campbell and Balfour came to the conclusion that the only way to save the club was to find a major backer willing to buy Newcastle Gosforth. The only man who filled the bill in the North-East was Sir John Hall.

Campbell and Balfour decided they would sound out Newcastle United's millionaire chairman to see if he was interested. They asked fellow Scot Duncan Madsen, a former Gosforth player and a local journalist, to ask his colleague John Gibson to approach Sir John Hall and ask him if he was interested. Sir John, who had long dreamed of a Newcastle Sporting Club encompassing many sports, answered in the affirmative and launched into a week's secret negotiations involving Campbell, Balfour and Newcastle United directors Douglas Hall, Sir John's son, and Freddie Shepherd.

So it was that on 5 September 1995 the news that shook the rugby world to its core was announced – Sir John Hall had bought Newcastle Gosforth. The shock waves ran worldwide and started rugby on a roller-coaster ride that shows no signs of slowing down. It transformed Newcastle Gosforth from a struggling second division side on the slide towards oblivion into Newcastle Falcons, who were to become Premiership champions within two years, Tetley's Bitter Cup finalists and one of the biggest rugby clubs in Britain, if not Europe. It also brought one of the biggest names in England rugby, Rob Andrew, back to the North-East as the man to head up Sir John Hall's new acquisition. Andrew's name was among those being bandied about within hours of the announcement from the St James' Park boardroom. The rumour mill moved into top gear and its pace has hardly slackened since. Besides Andrew, players who were already on their way, if you believed half of what was said and written, included Will Carling and the rest of the England team. It was, in fact, much of the Scottish team and further down the road a couple of former All Blacks, a few England internationals and five future British Lions.

At that press conference in St James' Park, Sir John Hall underlined why he had decided to take over Newcastle Gosforth: 'The rugby venture came right out of the blue in the last few days but it fits in perfectly with the way we are going. There are huge advantages to both parties and it puts us years ahead of the rest of the rugby world.' The takeover of Newcastle Gosforth was by Sir John in reality, but in name by the Newcastle Sporting Club which was backed by Cameron Hall Developments, Sir John Hall's main company. The Sporting Club acquired 76 per cent of the shares in the new company, Newcastle

RFC, with Newcastle Gosforth members holding the other 24 per cent.

The takeover was eventually completed with less controversy and argument than might have been expected. The vast majority of the Newcastle Gosforth members were realistic enough to see that it was the only way forward for their club, although a vocal minority made their views and opposition to the takeover known. It would have been surprising, though, if there had not been opposition in some quarters.

Newcastle Gosforth president Godfrey Clark described it as '...an historic merger. We are an ambitious club,' he told *The Journal*, Newcastle's morning paper, and added: 'We want to regain our first division status and then become the best club in the country. We could not achieve that without a substantial input of funds. Newcastle United have provided the funds, the financial clout and the marketing expertise.'

David Campbell also revealed that the decision to go to Newcastle United and Sir John Hall had not been a difficult one: 'Rugby is at a crossroads. We could have worked hard to stand still but in the current climate standing still would mean, in effect, going backwards. Instead we decided to go forward and opened negotiations with Newcastle United a week ago. We intend to get to the top quickly and dominate the rugby scene in this country. We are two years ahead of the field and we want to do for the rugby club what Kevin Keegan has done for the football club. We will be bringing in high profile players and they will certainly be of the stature of Will Carling and Rob Andrew.'

Newcastle United had been looking at entering Rugby League and were still investigating the possibility of a Super League franchise when they took on Newcastle Gosforth. While Sir John insisted for some time that it was still an option, he soon became one of the Falcons' biggest fans and the idea of a Rugby League side was eventually shelved quietly. Ironically, that did make it easier for the eventual birth of Gateshead Thunder and their short-lived one-season tenure at Gateshead International Stadium before they deserted to Hull.

The transfer of ownership from Newcastle Gosforth members to Newcastle Sporting Club was conducted at breakneck speed and with a facility which almost beggared belief. It is fair to say, though, that it might not have been so easy had the Newcastle Gosforth club's constitution not allowed the negotiations between Sir John and the Newcastle Gosforth board of management to proceed with too much recourse to the club membership. Having said that, the board of management, led by Ken Lockerbie, did negotiate increased representation for the club in the form of two directors instead of one on the Newcastle RFC five-man board and also valuable founder-member rights for the Newcastle Gosforth '24 per centers', as they quickly became known.

While the legalese to bring Newcastle Gosforth under the umbrella of the Newcastle Sporting Club was being sorted out, the Newcastle Gosforth players watched in amazement. The changes did precious little for coach Harry Patrick and his side in terms of results and they lost their opening Courage Division Two game at Moseley 9-0. However, they pulled themselves together and were able to concentrate for their first home game of the season, against Nottingham, and managed a good 31-24 win on 16 September.

If the Newcastle Gosforth players were amazed by the turn of events the first week in September, then they were completely gobsmacked when Rob Andrew walked through the door of the boardroom at St James' Park and was unveiled as their new Director of

Rugby on 21 September 1995.

Speculation had been rife since Newcastle United's takeover that Andrew was on his way, but many names had surfaced as possible alternatives. These included Barry Corless, whom Newcastle Gosforth had tried to lure to the North-East earlier, Keith Richardson, Roger Uttley, Ian McGeechan and Alan Black, another former Gosforth player and ex-Wasp now working for the RFU. Black was the favoured choice of many of the Newcastle Gosforth established guard as they knew him from his playing days with the club and while he played and coached at Wasps. Both Campbell and Balfour believed he could do the job for Newcastle, but Sir John had other ideas. He had already asked, who was the best man for the job? Who would have the respect of players? Who would have the business acumen and ability to lure players to Newcastle? In short, who could become the Kevin Keegan of rugby? The answer he was invariably given was Rob Andrew.

This sparked a 'let's get our man' chase by Freddie Shepherd and Douglas Hall. They contacted Andrew within twenty-four hours of Sir John's takeover of the club. Secret negotiations with Andrew and his agent were held in London and the deal to bring England's most capped fly-half to the North-East was completed in under two weeks. During the negotiations Andrew did actually visit the North-East to play at Barnard Castle, his former school, in a charity match along with Rory and Tony Underwood. Although he fended off questions about his future and a move to Newcastle with the dexterity journalists have come to know well, Andrew did say that he admired what Sir John Hall was trying to do at Newcastle. Those who left Barnard Castle School that day were convinced that Andrew had or was on the verge of accepting Sir John's overtures.

All the speculation disappeared on the morning of Thursday 21 September when the Wasps, England and British Lions fly-half walked through the door to assume the role of

Rob Andrew and Sir John Hall kick-start the Falcons at St James' Park. The Newcastle United chairman unveils Andrew as his man to head up the new Newcastle club following the takeover of Newcastle Gosforth by the Newcastle Sporting Club.

What advice do you have Kevin? Rob Andrew meets Newcastle United manager Kevin Keegan shortly after his appointment as Newcastle Falcons boss.

Director of Rugby of the country's first professional rugby club. The RFU may have vainly been trying to close the stable door after the horse had bolted by insisting on a moratorium on professionalism, but the days of amateur (or should that be shamateur) rugby at the top end of the English game were gone forever and Newcastle were leading the way.

Newcastle United would not reveal any financial details of their new Director of Rugby's contract and neither would Andrew, although it was a five-year contract and widely believed to be worth £750,000. This was big enough to persuade Andrew to give up a lucrative business career in the City of London.

An elated Sir John was in his element: 'Rob will do for the game of rugby in the North-East what Kevin Keegan has done for football. He is an inspirational appointment for a club that is going places,' he said as he indulged in an impromptu game of rugby with Andrew on the St James' Park pitch. Andrew was scheduled to start his new role as saviour of Newcastle Gosforth in October and said he would be moving to Newcastle with his family as soon as possible. 'I see this as a huge opportunity for us all to help lead North-East rugby back to the top where it should be – the game has huge potential here,' he said. 'We aim to become one of the top clubs in Europe and I am thrilled to be joining Newcastle at such an exciting time for Rugby Union. I have been attracted by Sir John's vision for the development of Rugby Union in the North-East as part of the Newcastle United Sporting Club.'

Andrew admitted to being in a slight state of shock over the turn of events that had dramatically changed his life and which was also to end his illustrious England career within a short space of time. 'It was only two weeks after Sir John Hall bought Newcastle Gosforth and there I was standing at St James' Park as the club's new Director of Rugby,' he said. 'It was twenty-four hours after the first moves to buy the club that Sir John, Douglas and Freddie contacted me and I spoke to them twenty-four hours later.'

It was Shepherd who made the first contact: 'We told him of our plans and Sir John's vision and it hit him right between the eyes,' he said. 'Sir John said go and get him and we did. Once we realised the deal with the rugby club could be done, we thought about who we would want and we thought of Rob as the man who could do for rugby what Kevin Keegan has done for football in Newcastle.'

And just what did the Newcastle Gosforth players think? To a man they applauded the move, although in their heart of hearts some of them must have known that it was now going to be a lot tougher at Kingston Park with the big names being talked about on their way: for some of them it was going to be the end of their Newcastle Gosforth careers. 'It's the second best thing that's happened to Newcastle rugby,' said Steve Douglas, 'the first was the rugby club becoming part of Sir John Hall's Sporting Club dream.'

After being unveiled as the new man at the Newcastle Gosforth helm, Andrew flew back to London and an uncertain immediate future with Wasps because of the complications caused by the 120-day registration rule. Although he had signed for Newcastle Gosforth as their Director of Rugby, Rob Andrew was also now a Newcastle player, but he would not be eligible to play for his new club until January due to that 120-day registration. He would be able to play for Wasps during that period but the question was, would they want him to? If he wasn't playing for Wasps' first team for four months, what consequences would that have for the thirty-two-year-old's England international career? It was to have the severest

Rob Andrew meets up with the Newcastle Gosforth players within days of settling into the Kingston Park hot seat. From left to right: Newcastle club captain Ross Wilkinson, Scottish international Richard Cramb, Rob Andrew, Richard Metcalfe, who was to play for Scotland, Paul Van-Zandvliet.

of consequences as matters came to a head the following month.

Meanwhile, Andrew's arrival on Tyneside sent shock waves throughout the country and also on Teesside, where West Hartlepool Director of Rugby Barry Forster said: 'The news represents a threat to every other club. We may be just down the road geographically to Newcastle but the threat is no less great to clubs like Leicester and Bath, and Wasps have just found out how easy it is to take someone away from you.' Forster added that he hoped Newcastle and West could live together 'like Everton and Liverpool' but his first words were prophetic as he immediately lost out on signing three Newcastle players: Richard Arnold, Richard Metcalfe and Peter Walton.

All three were having second thoughts about their proposed move to Brierton Lane in the wake of Andrew's signing and, in the end, none of the trio did go to West. Richard Arnold admits that one moment of recklessness on the field probably saved his Newcastle career. Fed up with the fact that Newcastle Gosforth appeared to be going nowhere but down the leagues, Arnold had signed a registration form for West Hartlepool, who were still in the First Division having narrowly escaped relegation in April. This meant that his 120-day registration period covered the summer and he was eligible for West in September, the start of the season.

> I'd signed for West because I wanted to play first division rugby and Gosforth were in the second flight,' said Arnold. 'I did the deal in April and served my 120-day registration period during the summer. But I'd been sent off in the last match of the season for Gosforth and had to sit out a 45-day

Richard Metcalfe (left) and Richard Arnold (with ball) quickly changed their minds about a move to West Hartlepool when Rob Andrew took over. Metcalfe, the giant lock, stayed on for the Falcons promotion and championship seasons but then moved on to Northampton and eventually Edinburgh Reivers, where he has flourished while Arnold is still with the Newcastle club.

Peter Walton in happy mood after deciding he would also be staying at Kingston Park and not moving to West Hartlepool following the arrival of Rob Andrew.

ban. It was during this period that Rob Andrew joined Newcastle and uttered words which were from heaven – he wanted me at Kingston Park. We had a couple of meetings, agreed terms, and I signed a week before I was due at West. But for my ban it would have been very different – I would have missed out on all the great times, including my testimonial.

There's no doubt that Andrew, desperate to steady a rocking boat, saw Arnold as one of his mainstays and he remembered Arnold from when he'd played for Wasps against Newcastle Gosforth, describing him as 'a bloody nuisance!' It's a description Arnold took as a compliment: 'I did try to take his head off, as so many opponents have, but failed.' Arnold's decision to stay was one of the best he made and Walton (now retired because of a neck problem and on the club's coaching staff) and Metcalfe would also change their minds about moving as Andrew set about bringing some of the top names in rugby to Newcastle.

As Andrew moved into Kingston Park on 2 October 1995, the club was on the move as well, but in the wrong direction – towards the bottom of Division Two. Defeats by Wakefield and Bedford dropped them to fourth bottom in the table and the new Director of Rugby knew he had a major task on his hands. 'I just want to get my feet under the table and get the feel of things,' he said on his first day in charge. 'Obviously I have ideas about how we should do things and the direction in which we should go, but it's a question of talking to people and all of us working together' he added, as rumours continued to fly about who would and would not be coming to Tyneside.

7
ANDREW PLUNDERS THE MARKET

Just who would be tempted to Kingston Park by Rob Andrew and Sir John's chequebook? The answer was just about any player of stature in the world and Newcastle very quickly became the most maligned and feared club in Britain. No one was safe as Wasps, the club Andrew was leaving to join Newcastle, were about to find out. However, one of Andrew's first signings after he and Sir John Hall met with the Newcastle players and explained their plans at a two-hour meeting was fairly low-key and straightforward. England 'A' centre Graham Childs, a former Wasps team-mate of Andrew, moved from West Hartlepool, but Wasps' worst fears were realised when Andrew moved in to sign their captain Dean Ryan on a three-year contract.

The arrival of the man Andrew described as an 'out-and-out winner' was a key part of the Newcastle player-manager's plans and Ryan was to play a major role in the Falcons' climb to the top as skipper and forwards coach. Like Andrew, Ryan was unable to play for his new club immediately because of the 120-day eligibility rule. It's an understatement to say Wasps were not best pleased at losing Ryan but what followed was, from their point of view, even worse, as Andrew persuaded both Ireland and British Lions prop Nick Popplewell and England 'A' scrum-half Steve Bates to leave the London club for Newcastle. Bates joined the Falcons as player-coach to form an impressive management triumvirate with Ryan and Andrew.

The departures prompted Wasps to ask Andrew and Ryan to leave the club immediately and not wait until their registration period had been completed. In effect, this was a decision that

Graham Childs was Rob Andrew's first official signing for Newcastle. Andrew's former Wasps' team-mate agreed to a move from West Hartlepool within days of Andrew arriving at Kingston Park.

The signing of Dean Ryan (above) for Newcastle, along with that of Steve Bates (right) and Nick Popplewell, caused an uproar at Wasps. Both Ryan and Rob Andrew were asked to leave the London club before the end of their registration period, which prompted Andrew to retire from international rugby as he would be kicking his heels for four months before he could play for Newcastle.

ended Andrew's England international career. Unable to play First Division rugby with Wasps and ineligible to turn out for his new club Newcastle until he had completed the 120-day registration period, Andrew decided he wouldn't wait to see if England manager Jack Rowell would prolong his international career. He announced his retirement from the England scene on 19 October 1995, although there was to be a swansong for England's most capped fly-half.

Andrew told the world's media at the time of his 'great regret' at having decided to retire from international rugby. Andrew insisted that Wasps' decision to exclude both him and Dean Ryan from club selection raised too many problems. 'I felt I must remove any further speculation about my England future and I did not want my appointment with Newcastle to cause any unnecessary damage to England's prospects,' said Andrew. While many regretted

Andrew's decision to call it a day with England, there were others who applauded his decision. Among them was Sir John Hall, who said 'England's loss is Newcastle's gain' and rejoiced in the fact that Andrew could concentrate fully on his role as Newcastle's player-manager. Andrew did that with increasing pace, completing the signing of Steve Bates and lining up England wing Tony Underwood, as well as Scottish and British Lions duo Doddie Weir and Gary Armstrong. Andrew described Armstrong as 'probably the best scrum-half in the world, a quality player and a quality individual'.

The signing of Weir and Armstrong was a real coup, although the Scottish pair were the victims of a classic Sir John Hall snow job. They had been invited down for talks with Andrew and Sir John and to have a look at the lie of the land when they suddenly found themselves wheeled into a St James' Park press conference with Underwood and presented as new signings. Technically, they had still to agree terms when they were unveiled on 1 November but within four weeks Armstrong was making his Newcastle debut against a touring Transvaal side, which attracted a crowd of nearly 3,500. Armstrong made it clear after the match that he and Weir expected to sign contracts 'within a matter of weeks', although it was to be January before Weir did finally agree terms.

Armstrong admits he looks back with gratitude to the day he and Weir were unveiled as new signings – even though they hadn't agreed a deal! 'Doddie and I only came down to have a look round – it was our first visit – but a press conference was being held to unveil Tony Underwood and we were conned into taking part even though we hadn't signed. When we got back in the car to drive home we heard the announcement on the radio and wondered what we'd done! Rob came up to Otterburn for a meeting a fortnight later and that's when I actually joined the Falcons. Doddie was later still.'

Armstrong, who was once described by Andrew as 'pound for pound, by far and away Newcastle's best player,' was to become the mainstay of the Falcons promotion drive and the

Sir John Hall listens intently as Rob Andrew announces to the media at a St James' Park press conference that Gary Armstrong (far left), Tony Underwood (left) and Doddie Weir (right) are to join the Falcons.

Can't wait to wear it. Tony Underwood displays the number fourteen shirt that he would wear with distinction for the Newcastle Falcons after signing for Rob Andrew and the Tynesiders from Leicester.

Nice isn't it? Gary Armstrong (left) and Doddie Weir take in the sights at St James' Park after being announced as new signings. They hadn't actually said yes or put pen to paper when Sir John Hall and Rob Andrew wheeled them out with Tony Underwood, but both went on to pledge their future to the club.

bedrock of their Premiership triumph. 'I came to Newcastle because the club is geared to the big time and I wanted a crack at the top club competition in rugby,' says Armstrong, who once drove a lorry for up to twelve hours a day in pursuit of a decent living wage. He often got up at 5.15 a.m. in the small border town of Jedburgh and returned home in time to be at rugby training with his local club at 7.00 p.m. 'I sometimes have to pinch myself when I realise what's happened. Professional rugby came at just the right time for me. If Newcastle hadn't chased my signature I'd probably have given up the game for family reasons and because there wasn't anything else for me to achieve. Jed Forest were in the relegation zone and I didn't know what to do. I'd moved to stand-off, then centre, then back to scrum-half. When I arrived in Newcastle, the club were fighting relegation from the second division but we went on to win promotion the next season, lifted the championship in our first year in the top flight and then reached the Tetley's Bitter Cup final. Newcastle has been perfect for me – and Rob Andrew sold me a dream that has come true. I'll be thirty-five when my contract with Newcastle is up and that'll probably be it,' said the man who captained Scotland to the last Five Nations Championship trophy.

Armstrong's club debut for Newcastle was on 28 November 1995 along with Dean Ryan, and with Andrew making his debut against Harrogate in a league game three days earlier, it was the start of a new era for the Newcastle club. Newcastle defeated Harrogate 51-5 in that match at Kingston Park and Andrew kicked two penalties, six conversions and a drop goal as Newcastle cruised to their best win of the season with Graham Childs and Nick Popplewell also in the side. Tony Underwood and Dean Ryan followed them into Newcastle's League line-up in the New Year, which was to bring a period of startling change at Kingston Park.

Rob Andrew runs out at Kingston Park to make his Newcastle League debut against Harrogate.

British Lion Scott Gibbs was linked with a possible move to the North-East but it was West Hartlepool captain Tim Stimpson who was to prove the next capture for Andrew. The England full-back decided on a move to Newcastle after offers from Leicester, a club he would eventually move on to after he became increasingly unsettled at Kingston Park. 'Moving to Newcastle wasn't about money,' said Stimpson. 'I signed for the club because I felt it was where I could develop as a player and I wanted to be part of club that was obviously going to go places. It was still the hardest decision I have ever had to make because I had two great years at West and they developed me from the university player into an England player and they looked after me very well.'

New signings were made at breakneck speed and no sooner had Stimpson completed his move to Newcastle on 4 April than Andrew was unveiling a hat-trick of new players in Ross Nesdale, Garath Archer and Andrew Blyth two weeks later. South Shields-born Archer was son of Gosforth winger Stewart, who played in the 1981 John Player Cup final. He had been playing for Bristol, a club he would eventually return to at the start of the 1999/2000 season with Falcons skipper Dean Ryan. Blyth was a local lad born in Hexham, but educated at Rugby School, who had been playing for West Hartlepool after leaving Tynedale. Blyth, who played for England 'A', later moved on to Harlequins, Northampton and Sale, where, sadly, he suffered a serious back injury in the 1999/2000 season which ended his playing career.

It was the signing of Ross Nesdale that raised a few eyebrows. However, it proved to be a very astute acquisition by Andrew, who was the first to admit there was an element of luck involved. New Zealander Nesdale was looking for a move to England, and Newcastle were the first club to respond to the video and CV he sent out. Nesdale, understudy to All Black hooker and captain Sean Fitzpatrick, was also the holder of an Irish passport and he was to go on and play for Ireland in the Five Nations Championship. A graduate in business studies and

England full-back Tim Stimpson (left) joins up with boss Rob Andrew and Tony Underwood (right) after becoming another Newcastle capture from West Hartlepool.

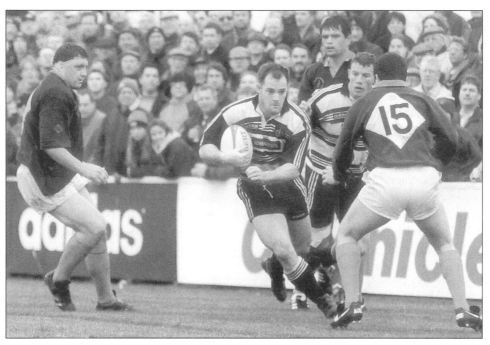

Rob Andrew made a hat-trick of signings when he secured the services of England second row Garath Archer, Ross Nesdale (above) and Andy Blyth, but the Kiwi hooker was a real bonus. Newcastle snapped him up after he contacted the club with his CV and he turned out to be a real capture.

67

a qualified graphic artist, Nesdale is not your average hooker. In fact, his intelligent approach to the game allied with typical New Zealand grit quickly made him a firm favourite with the Kingston Park faithful and an integral part of the Falcons side which was to win promotion and the Premiership title.

Further signings came in the shape of George Graham from Carlisle Rugby League Club, Steve O'Neill from local side Blaydon and Martin Shaw from West Hartlepool. With a core of players still remaining from the pre-takeover days, notably Ross Wilkinson, Martin Wilson, Neil Frankland, Steve Douglas and Paul Van-Zandvliet, Andrew believed he had a squad capable of winning promotion from Division Two. The spectre of relegation had been removed towards the end of the 1995/96 season with the news that the Courage Leagues would be expanded. This enabled West Hartlepool to avoid the drop to Division Two, despite finishing bottom, because the top division increased to twelve clubs and there was no relegation that season. Newcastle would not have gone down, regardless of the decision to also scrap relegation from Division Two, because they finished third from bottom on points difference from Nottingham and Bedford with 5 wins and a draw in their 18 games. Nevertheless, it was a narrow escape and everyone connected with the Newcastle club knew it.

George Graham was another significant addition to the Newcastle squad. Virtually unknown, he came to the club on the suggestion of Dean Ryan, with whom he had served in the Army. Graham, a pocket battleship, would establish himself as one of the Falcons' leading players and would be capped for Scotland. He was voted Premiership player of the 1999/2000 season by the 24 percenters and local morning paper *The Journal* in their Keith Pattinson Journal Trophy awards.

One man who was to prove a crucial figure was fitness adviser Steve Black, who was seconded from Newcastle United, where he had been working with Kevin Keegan on conditioning the soccer stars. Black's presence at Kingston Park was a real stroke of luck for the Falcons. He immediately hit it off with Rob Andrew, Steve Bates and Dean Ryan and his ideas on training, fitness and conditioning fitted in with the triumvirate's plans and aspirations. Black quickly became a central figure, a father-confessor to the players and a vital cog in the Newcastle machine. It was quickly evident that Black had something special, an unusual rapport with the players and he was able to get the best out of them in the most extreme circumstances. He would also protect them from themselves and the demands put on them by club and country. He knew instinctively when a player needed a break or to rest, or if something was wrong. It is doubtful whether Newcastle would have won the Premiership the season after they won promotion, had it not been for Steve Black's ability to keep the players fresh and firing on all cylinders. His revolutionary and, at times, unconventional approach prompted sneers in some quarters, but Newcastle were always fitter, faster and more organised than other sides. They kept their edge as they rampaged through the Second Division and then took the Premiership title.

When Black was tempted away to become Wales' fitness adviser by Graham Henry, it was significant that Newcastle went through an awful season. Although there were mitigating circumstances of a horrendous injury situation and World Cup calls, the absence of Black was keenly felt. Happily, that situation was remedied towards the end of the 1999/2000 season when Black, often nicknamed Pavarotti because of his likeness to the opera star and his belief that he could sing as well, returned from Wales to resume his position with the Falcons.

8
FALCONS TAKE FLIGHT

Newcastle's build up to the new season started with a tour to South Africa. With a new name and a new black and white strip, Newcastle Falcons played matches against Western Transvaal, Gruiqualand West and South-Eastern Transvaal.

The tour was to give the players a chance to bond and to get to know each other on and off the field. It was also a hard learning curve for the Newcastle squad, who lost 36-33 in their opening game against Western Transvaal and then went down 31-6 to Griqualand West before drawing 24-24 with South-East Transvaal. Only some hometown refereeing decisions denied Newcastle a victory in their final match, but there is no doubt that the object of the tour was a success because the Falcons' players went to South Africa as a bunch of individuals and came back a team. Eight hours in a bus travelling across the High Veldt saw to that, as did visiting places like Potchefstroom, Kimberley and Johannesburg. They were also provided with dinner in a prison, where it was their pleasure to be served by inmates, some of them serving sentences of life imprisonment for murder – none of them for poisoning fortunately! It was real, gritty, down-to-earth rugby and learning to get on with each other, although there was plenty of light relief provided by Irishman David Quinn, who discovered a source of fireworks and a rare talent for setting them off in the most amazing places. There was also a visit to the Johannesburg branch of the Newcastle United supporters club!

On their return to the UK there was another draw for the Falcons, 26-26 at Melrose, and, clearly, there was a lot of work ahead before they could be considered the finished article. Victory by 30-13 in their opening Division Two game on 7 September 1996 failed to dispel doubts among the crowd of 2,000 at Kingston Park, although Andrew delighted the faithful by scoring one of the four tries. Many of the doubts disappeared in the Falcons' second match when they hammered Nottingham 74-29 away from home, scoring twelve tries.

Off the field there was plenty to keep the media occupied, with Newcastle in the thick of it. Louis Luyt, president of the South African Rugby Union, paid a flying visit to the North-East and was a guest of Newcastle chairman Sir John Hall at the Newcastle United versus Halmstad UEFA Cup-tie. Luyt was the man behind the deal which saw the birth of the Super 10s (now Super 12s) tournament in which the top provincial sides from South Africa, Australia and New Zealand play each other, and also the Tri-Nations Championship that involves the international sides of the same three Southern Hemisphere countries. Luyt brokered the deal between the South African, Australian and New Zealand Rugby Unions and Rupert Murdoch's News Corporation during the 1995 World Cup in South Africa, which led to the end of shamateurism and forced the International Board to declare the game of rugby open. It was apparent to Sir John Hall that the only way rugby in Britain and Europe could make itself successful in a commercial world was by selling itself to television, and the best way of doing this was by picking Louis Luyt's brains. Sir John was not a man to let opportunities pass him by or the chance to push back the boundaries and his attitude was that if this upset the officials at Twickenham, then so be it.

Sir John travelled to Scotland with Donald Kerr on behalf of English Professional Rugby Union Clubs (EPRUC), the forerunner of English First Division Rugby (EFDR), and met with leading club officials to outline plans for the future of European rugby under the umbrella of a European Rugby Federation. It was just one of the opening shots in what was to be a long-running war between the club owners and the national unions, especially the RFU, which was to wrack the game for the next five years and was one of the factors that eventually led to Sir John, his son Douglas and fellow United shareholder Freddie Shepherd cutting their ties with the Falcons. This plunged the club into a crisis that almost led to the club's closure before a new owner, David Thompson, stepped in to rescue the Falcons.

On the field in 1996/97, however, things were starting to happen with a 61-0 crushing of Blackheath and still more players being recruited. These included John Bentley, although in this case the player sold himself to the Falcons instead of the other way around. The former England Rugby Union international was playing Rugby League with Halifax, but made the switch of codes so successfully that he became a major part of Newcastle's promotion drive, was recalled to the England side and went on the successful British Lions tour to South Africa in 1997 – one of five Newcastle players to make trip. Bentley finished joint top try scorer on that Lions tour along with Tony Underwood, his Falcons wing colleague, and maintains that it was the highlight of his career.

Bentley knew that playing for Newcastle would put him in the England and Lions running and he used all his powers of persuasion to get Rob Andrew to take him on, something which the Newcastle player-manager was happy to do. Andrew also recognised what it meant to have high-profile players knocking on his door at Newcastle – Bentley would not be the last Rugby League player to do that. Alan Tait, who was, arguably, to have the biggest impact on

John Bentley and Alan Tait both realised the possibilities of playing Rugby League and Rugby Union now that the barriers were down and they literally sold themselves to Rob Andrew. Tait (right) especially was to play a major role in the Premiership title win and with Bentley (left) would play for the British Lions in 1997.

Newcastle's back play, followed the Bentley route and switched codes. He became the first player to return from Rugby League and be capped for Scotland, and also the first player to play for the Great Britain Rugby League side and then the British Lions Rugby Union team.

It was Bentley, however, who blazed the trail at Newcastle, quickly realising the possibilities after the game went open and the lines between the codes became blurred. 'I was lying in the bath at Harlequins after Halifax had beaten London Broncos when the enormity of the whole situation hit me,' said Bentley. 'Here I was at The Stoop, the bastion of Rugby Union clubs and I had just played a game of Rugby League there. Six months before, that would have been unheard of. After that nothing would ever surprise me again and then there I was playing Rugby Union with Newcastle Falcons after eight years of Rugby League. I went to League because I was disillusioned when I missed out on playing for the North after I felt I'd been the best centre in the county championship. I'd been approached by Rugby League clubs throughout my Union career and Leeds simply came in at the right time with the right offer and I never ever regretted the decision to go to League or the decision to switch back to Union with Newcastle.'

Newcastle may have been second division in name, but they were first division in terms of the quality of their squad. England manager Jack Rowell recognised that when he named full-back Tim Stimpson, wing Tony Underwood, centre Andrew Blyth and lock Garath Archer in his September squad to prepare for the international championship and pre-Christmas matches against Argentina and Italy. Rowell's plans had been disrupted by EPRUC ordering the clubs – including Newcastle – to withdraw their players from a previous squad session as the rift between the RFU and the clubs deepened. The crisis was never very far away from blazing into open warfare and both sides were guilty of airing their views in the media when they would have been better advised keeping their discussions behind closed doors.

The game was changing, whether people liked it or not, and the evidence was clear to see on the field as well with seventeen internationals taking the field at Richmond on 28 September 1996, when they met Newcastle in a Division Two game. Richmond had also been taken over by a new backer in millionaire Ashley Levett and had recruited assiduously in an attempt to catch up Newcastle, signing international players Ben Clarke and the Quinnell brothers, Scott and Craig, as well as Welshman Allan Bateman from Rugby League. The match ended in a 20-20 draw and it was the first of several big matches between the two clubs, with Richmond going on to prove a thorn in Newcastle's side throughout their Division Two campaign and then in the Premiership. After the match, Rob Andrew went on record as saying he was happy with his current squad but would not rule out further additions if the right player became available.

According to many reports, the player Andrew sought was French fly-half Thomas Castaignède. There's little doubt that Castaignède was ready for a move to England, but he was willing to play off the likes of Newcastle, Wasps, Harlequins and Saracens (also now big players in the professional game with Nigel Wray backing them) against each other.

Clearly, Newcastle were on the look out for a player to groom as a successor to Rob Andrew who, while not yet ready for the scrap heap, was thirty-three. They did have a young player whom they rated highly, who had joined the club for a year to 'see how things go'. His name was Jonny Wilkinson. The Castaignède saga was to run for some time, with the mercurial Frenchman fanning the flames of speculation when he admitted he could be influenced by the

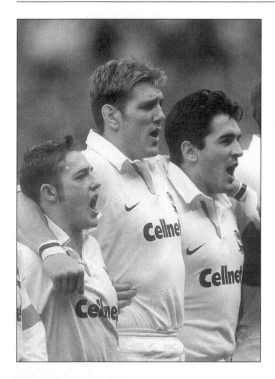

Proud to be English. Garath Archer was one of several Falcons called up for international duty by England manager Jack Rowell even though the club was in Division Two. Rowell knew that Newcastle were of First Division class in terms of playing personnel.

fact that David Ginola was playing for Newcastle United at the time. 'I don't know David personally,' said Castaignède, 'but he has settled well in Newcastle and I don't see why I couldn't as well. If my manager can sort things out I will be playing in England next season and Newcastle could be the answer. I want a club with ambitions to be the best.' The Castaignède deal never materialised, but the question is, did Rob Andrew and Steve Bates know even then that they had a player of rare quality in the shape of Jonny Wilkinson? The answer is most certainly yes, although Wilkinson's time was yet to come and Andrew, quite rightly, was at that time interested in players who were ready and available to do a job for the Falcons in Division Two.

Great Britain Rugby League full-back Alan Tait fell into that category. Somewhat surprisingly, Tait's Rugby League career at Leeds had stalled and he was desperate for a move. Although there were many difficulties with Tait's contract with both the Yorkshire club and with Super League, the player was determined and trained with Newcastle while badgering the life out of Andrew. Eventually a deal was struck and Andrew later admitted that it was one of the best he has ever made because Tait brought a real cutting edge to the Newcastle back line, a professional attitude to defence that was to prove vital and essential education for some of the Falcons' younger players.

Even if Tait's penchant for missing training during the week and suddenly being fit for the weekend match became a legendary joke among his team-mates, they quickly recognised Tait's ability to spot a gap and his lines of running were out of the top drawer. Scotland identified Tait's ability and it also didn't take British Lions manager Fran Cotton and Ian McGeechan long to realise it as well. They took him to South Africa in 1997, where he was one of the key figures in the Lions' 2-1 Test series win over the Springboks.

Reports that Newcastle were trying to sign French star Thomas Castaignède proved unfounded but they did bring a promising youngster to the club as they chased promotion. His name was Jonny Wilkinson.

The Lions was the main topic of conversation in rugby clubs the length and breadth of the land, but it was the Falcons' performance against Rugby Lions which pushed talk of South Africa and who would be in McGeechan's squad into the background. Disappointed with what they considered a dropped point at Richmond, Newcastle produced a shattering performance against Rugby. The Falcons established a Courage National League record with a 156-5 win, scoring 24 tries, 18 of which Andrew converted. After the match, the Newcastle manager said: 'We've ended up with a great bunch of lads capable of playing great rugby and the exciting thing is that we're only just starting. We have so much footballing ability right from one to fifteen and we have to let that shine through. We have to maintain this level week after week. Dean Ryan, Steve Bates and I have a vision of how we want to play the game. It doesn't always work week after week but we have to keep aiming for that and we were very disappointed with our performance at Richmond.'

Sir John Hall watched the match but much of his time was being spent on the increasingly bitter confrontation between the top clubs and national unions. There were almost daily rumours and reports of a possible breakaway from the RFU by the clubs to set up their own league. The recriminations and threats from both sides did the game's image no good at all and many players were naturally worried what it could mean for their international careers. Newcastle trio Doddie Weir, Gary Armstrong and Peter Walton had not yet signed contracts with the Scottish Rugby Union because of dispute over match fees, but the underlying problems concerned the issue of clubs releasing players for district and international matches, and the clash of dates with league games and internationals.

9
SAMOAN SWOOP

The changes at Kingston Park that professionalism had brought were about to cause one of the saddest rifts in the history of the club although, perversely, it would ensure the survival of the name Gosforth.

The Newcastle Falcons board of directors decided that they would no longer fund the running of the adult junior sides at Kingston Park – the second, third and fourth teams – which were largely made up of former senior players and those who played the game for fun and recreation. Instead, they would be concentrating on only their core sides: the Falcons, the Academy side and the Under 21/Colts squad. These changes led to many players and officials leaving Kingston Park to re-form the Gosforth club, basing themselves at Bullocksteads, the home of Northumbria University, and just a couple of hefty Rob Andrew kicks from Kingston Park. They reverted to the green and white hooped shirts of their predecessors.

The new club had to start at the bottom of the Courage League and was placed in Durham and Northumberland Division Four. It was not a happy departure and many ex-players and former Gosforth members still harbour resentment over the issue. The Falcons' current management admit that the situation was handled badly, as was the decision to effectively show the door to the club's mini-rugby and youth section by refusing to fund them as well. The mini-juniors moved in with Gosforth at Bullocksteads and happily both are flourishing. Strenuous efforts have been made by David Thompson, who took over as Newcastle's new owner from Sir John Hall, to re-establish friendly links with the Gosforth club, and there has been a definite improvement in relations between Newcastle Falcons and Gosforth and also with clubs in the North-East in general. However, at the time the Falcons' decision to divest themselves of the junior sides and mini-youth section prompted much ill-feeling locally and gave critics nationally plenty of ammunition to snipe at Sir John's 'cheque-book Newcastle side'.

The criticism that the Falcons received nationally certainly did much to forge team spirit and there was very much an attitude amongst the players of 'We're the new kids on the block and if you don't like us, we don't care'. This attitude and determination was evident in the way Newcastle played the game and was epitomised by skipper Dean Ryan and his insistence on his players never taking a backward step. It wasn't pretty at times, but it was effective as Wakefield found out when they were the next victims of the promotion campaign, going down 47-17.

Newcastle also showed that they were responsive to what other people in the game wanted from them. England manager Jack Rowell sent a plea to Andrew asking if Tim Stimpson, whom he had pencilled in as England's full-back in the upcoming match against Italy, could be given more chance to kick at goal, especially when Newcastle 'were up 100 points or more'. Andrew's reply was that Stimpson had to earn his chance by putting in the kicking practice! Stimpson did as he was asked and worked hard with Falcons, England and British

Lions kicking-coach Dave Alred. The practise paid off and Stimpson was handed the kicking role in Newcastle's 75-9 hammering of Moseley, a match that was watched by British Lions manager Fran Cotton.

There was more trouble brewing off the field when Newcastle learned that RFU had moved the goalposts again with regard to how many players needed to be on international duty before they could call off a league game. The initial rule had been that clubs could call off a league game if they had more than three players on international duty, but it had been subtly changed from 'players from the four home unions' to 'English-qualified players'. This meant that Newcastle's Scottish and Irish contingent were excluded from any calculation, leading to the possibility of the Falcons being unable to call off their league games against Rotherham and the return match against Richmond (which clashed with Scotland and Ireland games), and having to field a severely-weakened side. The implications for Newcastle's promotion hopes were enormous and there was even the farcical suggestion from RFU sources that Newcastle and Richmond (who also wanted the game postponed because of international calls) could be forced to play a match that could decide promotion for both clubs with understrength sides.

Andrew immediately made it clear that he reserved the right not to release his six internationals – Doddie Weir, Gary Armstrong, Peter Walton and George Graham to Scotland, and Nick Popplewell and Ross Nesdale to Ireland – unless there was a solution. Rotherham were refusing to switch the game after three weeks of discussions and they could hardly be blamed for that, seeing it as a possible opportunity of an upset against an understrength Newcastle side. All this took place against a background of the first blip in Newcastle's drive for promotion. Having established themselves as clear favourites to go up with a 49-12 over Bedford, they then lost 19-18 at Coventry and had John Bentley sent off for fighting in an ill-tempered game played in front of a hostile and vociferous 8,000 crowd. Bentley apologised to his team-mates after the game for losing his temper after he had been sorely provoked by being taken out off the ball several times and there was some sympathy for the situation in which he had been dismissed. The defeat allowed Richmond to go top of Division Two and the only good thing that came out of a black weekend was the postponement of the league game against Rotherham, following the Scottish RU putting massive pressure on the RFU and the International Board, who eventually sanctioned the game's postponement.

Newcastle's plans for the future of rugby in the North-East and for the Falcons were revealed when they announced the setting up of their new development programme with a Rugby Academy and the appointment of Paul MacKinnon, a New Zealander, as their youth development officer. It was an appointment that was to have far-reaching consequences for the future of the Falcons and is now widely regarded as one of the club's best decisions. One of Paul MacKinnon's first tasks was to hand over special bursaries to several promising young university players, among them Ross Beattie who would be capped for Scotland on their tour to New Zealand in the summer of 2000. 'Paul knows the game inside out,' said Andrew on his appointment, 'and his role will be manyfold but we want a rugby development scheme which works for rugby, for us and for the North-East. It's an investment for the future and I want our development side to be full of eighteen to twenty-year-olds looking to be going on to be full-time professional players.' Andrew's words were prophetic as the Falcons now have one of the finest under-21 academies in the country and their under-21 side were invited to tour New Zealand in summer 2000, the first time an under-21 side from the professional rugby club had been asked to do so.

While Andrew, Bates and Ryan were planning ahead to a time when the Falcons would nurture and produce their own talented youngsters, the Newcastle player-manager was back in the market, wheeling and dealing for new players. Alan Tait gained his release from Leeds, bringing the prospect of him joining the Falcons a step nearer, but Andrew was lining up a double coup. The targets were Va'aiga Tuigamala, another former Rugby League star, and Pat Lam, who was arguably to be Newcastle's finest signing. Tuigamala was on a short-term contact with Andrew's former club, Wasps, and the former All Black and Samoan star was all set to re-sign for the London club before Andrew flew to Dublin to watch him and Lam play for Samoa against Ireland. The deal took some time to finalise, but Andrew had made the right move at the right time.

Back in Newcastle, Tait was knocking on Andrew's door again having gained his release from Leeds and his Super League contract. 'We would like Alan to come here and he wants to come here, so it is just a question of sorting out the details,' said Andrew. The deal was finalised and Tait made a try-scoring debut against West Hartlepool on Sunday 15 December 1996. Another piece of the Premiership jigsaw was in place and so was the man who was to win an award as the team's biggest whinger on bus journeys!

Arguably Newcastle's best signing (apart from Jonny Wilkinson) was Pat Lam. Even though he was only with the club for a couple of seasons his impact was enormous and along with Dean Ryan he formed a formidable back row partnership.

While most attention had been centred on Tim Stimpson making his England debut against Italy, there was an international comeback for Rob Andrew when he was one of five Newcastle players asked to be part of the Barbarians squad for December's match against Australia, the side he had sent tumbling out of the World Cup in Cape Town with a stunning late drop goal. Doddie Weir, Gary Armstrong, Tony Underwood and Nick Popplewell were the other four Falcons asked to make themselves available. In the event, Stimpson was also called up to play alongside Andrew, Underwood and Popplewell with Armstrong and Weir on the replacements' bench.

Stimpson also decided to play for the Falcons against London Scottish in their Division Two match a week before his England debut, causing something of a stir in doing so but Stimpson was surprised by the fuss: 'To be honest, I never really thought of anything other than playing for Newcastle. I honestly didn't realise it was a tradition to sit out the game a week before your first cap. It's a professional game now and I'm employed by Newcastle and England, and there's no way you start playing one against the other. I could do with another game to build my confidence and I don't want to be thinking I have to walk on eggshells until the England game starts.' A laudable attitude and, fortunately, Stimpson wasn't injured in Newcastle's 28-12 win over London Scottish. In fact, he had a superb game, scoring a hat-trick of tries, which Newcastle were grateful for as they did not play well and wasted several chances. The win took Newcastle back into second spot in Division Two following the Coventry debacle.

Stimpson made a satisfactory England debut in England's 54-21 win over Italy and there was a nice gesture from Newcastle United skipper Peter Beardsley, who sent Stimpson a pre-match fax wishing him luck, as did Rob Andrew as well as former clubs West Hartlepool and Durham University. Stimpson was rewarded for his solid display by being named in the England side against New Zealand Barbarians and for the Barbarians against Australia a week later. England lost 34-19 to the New Zealand Barbarians, who were no less than the All Blacks under another name, and Stimpson was one of the few players to emerge with credit. He also played for the Barbarians against Australia but suffered concussion while tackling Aussie winger David Campese. This kept him out of the England game against Argentina the following week when there was a recall for Newcastle wing Tony Underwood to the England side.

It was turning out to be a real season and half for the Falcons when they came out of the hat at home to neighbours West Hartlepool for the third round of the Pilkington Cup. However, there were already signs of disenchantment from Sir John Hall who was finding the labyrinthine world of rugby difficult to deal with after being used to making quick decisions in the business field and the world of soccer. Although an announcement was made late in November proclaiming (prematurely as it turned out) that English rugby's year-long feud was over with the hammering out of an agreement between EPRUC and the RFU, Sir John was not happy with the deal and Newcastle, along with Bedford, Saracens, Harlequins and Wasps, initially refused to sign the agreement because of a dispute over television and commercial rights. Sir John resigned as chairman of the Second Division clubs' organisation and from EPRUC. He also turned down the chance to sit on the new body being set up by the RFU and EPRUC to run the professional game because he did not agree with the RFU, saying they had the right to negotiate a deal on television rights. Sir John said he reserved the right to go to law if necessary to protect Newcastle's interests.

Refusing to sign the agreement raised the possibility of Newcastle's expulsion from the Courage Leagues and the RFU, a threat that was counter-productive at the time as the Falcons had every intention of signing up once they were sure of what the agreement meant, although the row did raise speculation over Newcastle Sporting Club's long-term commitment to the Falcons. Freddie Shepherd, one of three Newcastle United and Sporting Club directors on the Newcastle RFC board, tried to quash the speculation when he said, 'There's no way we would walk away from the rugby club. We're not quitters and never will be. We're not short-term merchants.' Newcastle did eventually sign the EPRUC and RFU agreement in the February of 1997.

Meanwhile, Alan Tait made his long-awaited debut for Newcastle in a friendly match – if there is ever such a thing – at West Hartlepool, a game played just a week before the two sides were due to meet in the Pilkington Cup. Newcastle won the game 29-13 and Tait scored but it had little relevance to the cup-tie, which Newcastle went into as clear favourites against a West Hartlepool side struggling on and off the field with the revelation that they had plunged £500,000 into the red and were facing a demand for repayment of a £200,000 loan by May. They had to sell their Brierton Lane ground, spent a season sharing with Hartlepool United, the town's soccer club, and slipped from the First Division to the Third Division in successive seasons.

Nearly 5,000 people turned up at Kingston Park for the Pilkington Cup-tie and West were thrashed 51-10 to raise genuine hopes of a league and cup double for the Falcons. There was also much talk about the need for Kingston Park to be upgraded to handle crowds of 8 to 10,000. A 39-15 win at London Scottish in the sixth round of the cup fanned the flames of cup fever at Newcastle, especially when they were drawn at home to Leicester in the quarter-finals which prompted speculation the match might be played at St James' Park.

Rob Andrew, meanwhile, was on the verge of an amazing double swoop for Samoans Pat Lam and Va'aiga Tuigamala. The Newcastle manager had attended the Ireland versus Samoa match the previous November and had secret talks with Lam when he flew him in to Newcastle. The deal was eventually finalised the following month, but things started to move at pace with regard to Tuigamala only when Newcastle realised he was available and approached Wigan. Tuigamala had moved back to Rugby League with Wigan after a short-term contract at Wasps, but there were many problems which Andrew had to surmount to sign the former All Blacks wing. These included the loyalty bonus paid to all Super League players by Rupert Murdoch's News Corporation, the fee that Wigan wanted and also the Samoan's personal terms. While negotiations were proceeding to bring Tuigamala to Kingston Park, Andrew caught everyone on the hop again by completing the signing of Tuigamala's Samoan friend and team-mate Pat Lam. 'I had a few offers when we were over in the UK on tour,' said Lam, 'but what stood out most was that Rob flew me over to Newcastle after the Irish match and I had a look around and I was so impressed with the whole set-up. The thing that also really impressed me was that Rob, before talking money, talked to me about the whole vision of where the club was aiming to go and the five-year plan he had and that appealed to me the most. To be part of team very similar to Samoa, working its way up was just what I wanted. If it had been just about money I would have gone somewhere else.'

Not even a week of wind and rain after his arrival on Tyneside could dampen Lam's spirits and he quickly became a member of the Toon Army after he was taken to his first-ever soccer match at St James's Park and learned in a short space of time the Geordie passion for sport. 'I'd been to England a few times and I had been up in Newcastle before and I was always interested in coming over to England and so did my wife Steph.' Lam got in touch with Newcastle's New Zealand hooker Ross Nesdale, whom he played alongside for Auckland, before deciding to make the move to the Falcons. Nesdale told Lam just what a top side Newcastle could become and what a great place the North-East is. 'He told me his wife Joanna had settled in really well and I knew we would have no difficulty in adjusting to life on Tyneside.'

Lam was as good as his word and he quickly became a great favourite with the Falcons fans and there was no doubt he was looking for somewhere to put down roots. 'I nearly quit rugby because 1995 was an absolute horror year,' said Lam. 'I was in South Africa for five weeks at the beginning of the year, came home for two weeks to see my son Bryson born before I was back in South Africa for another five weeks for the World Cup. Then I was in the Pacific for three weeks and spent eight weeks in the UK later that year – it was ridiculous. Being away so much was putting strain on the family so I had decided to retire from rugby.' But fortunately for the Falcons, rugby turned professional and Lam was able to give up his job as a teacher and to take up rugby full time. The move to Newcastle was a natural progression for Lam and he signed a two and half year contract and was to play a major role in Newcastle's Premiership success. Sadly, the Samoan powerhouse was not to stay with Newcastle long after that, moving on to Northampton in another transfer deal that would shock rugby, and which is still the subject of much controversy and debate among Newcastle followers.

Lam's arrival at Kingston Park dramatically increased the possibility of Tuigamala completing a move to the North-East as he and Lam were, and still are, great friends. Jack Robinson, the Wigan chairman, all but conceded that Wigan were about lose their star player on 13 February 1997 after he had talks with the player and Wigan's operations manager David Bradshaw said, 'We have told Newcastle we will get back to them as quickly as possible bearing in mind the rugby union transfer deadline.' Andrew had put together a package believed to be worth around £1m for Tuigamala, paying Wigan £500,000 for the player, the £180,000 loyalty bonus which had to be paid back to Super League and Tuigamala's personal terms. Wigan were £3.3m in debt at the time and trying to sell Central Park to supermarket giants Tesco as well as well as trying to offload players. Lam made his debut in Newcastle's 70-8 win at Rugby Lions on 8 February 1997 and, not surprisingly, scored a try.

Newcastle's growing influence on the national stage was reflected by the fact that four Falcons were on the pitch at Twickenham for that February's Calcutta Cup and Five Nations match with Tim Stimpson at full-back for England and Tony Underwood on the wing, while Doddie Weir and Peter Walton were in the Scotland pack. It echoed the 1977 Calcutta Cup match when Roger Uttley, Malcolm Young and Peter Dixon played for England and Duncan Madsen for Scotland, and there were a record six Newcastle players on full international duty that weekend in 1997 with Nick Popplewell and Ross Nesdale in the Ireland front row against Wales.

February 1997 was a watershed month in Newcastle's history because, by the end of it, Va'aiga Tuigamala was a Falcons player having moved from Wigan in a £1m deal, signing a five-year contract. It was a breathtakingly audacious swoop and confirmed Newcastle as the biggest player in the professional game. Yet it was only a fortunate combination of

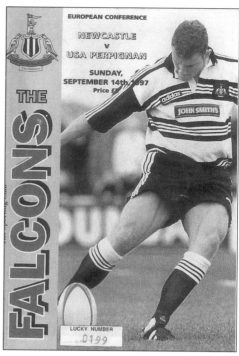

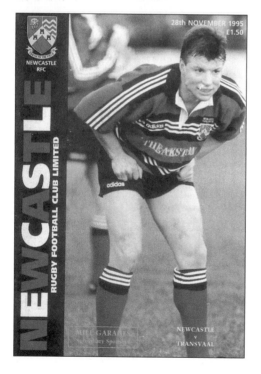

*Clockwise from left:
The changing style of
Newcastle programmes
from 1995 to 2000.*

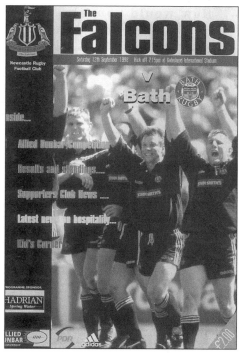

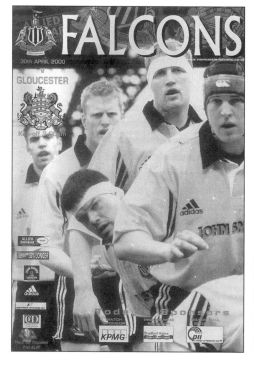

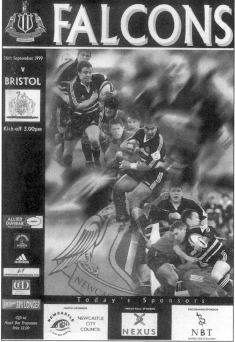

circumstances that led to Tuigamala making the move to Kingston Park – manager Rob Andrew talked of a 'window of opportunity' which opened to allow the deal. Andrew and his right-hand men, Steve Bates and Dean Ryan, had been thinking about the possibility of making a couple of additional signings after Coventry had exposed a lack of genuine pace in the Newcastle back row and problems in midfield. Great Britain Rugby League star Alan Tait had been lined up and eventually signed but the trio felt there was still a need for a big, powerful centre and a pacy back row forward. As the Samoans were just about to start their tour of Britain and Ireland, the trio decided to run the rule over the possibilities.

Bates and Ryan drove down to Oxford to watch the Oxford University v. Samoa match and talked to two of the Samoans – a back row forward and an inside centre. The back row forward was, of course, Pat Lam, while the centre was To'o Vaega. Both were interested in joining Newcastle and Andrew flew to Dublin to watch them play, and beat, Ireland 40-25. Although Tuigamala made his debut for Samoa in that match, he was not thought to be available as he was playing for Wasps on a short-term contract as well as rugby league for Wigan. Lam and Vaega subsequently came to see Andrew at Kingston Park, liked what they saw and agreed to join subject to release from their contracts in New Zealand. Lam was released but Vaega was not and that left Andrew with a spot still to fill in his back line. It was then Newcastle directors Douglas Hall and Freddie Shepherd asked Andrew, 'Of all the players in the world, who would you like most?' Andrew's reply was: 'There's only one – Va'aiga Tuigamala', to which Hall and Shepherd said, 'Well, why don't you see if you can get him, then!' A phone call to Tuigamala's agent David McKnight was made and it was just in time because Wasps had approached Wigan with a complicated offer involving a near £3m interest-free loan to the cash-strapped league club in return for Inga playing rugby union for Wasps and rugby league for Wigan for the next three years. Tuigamala wasn't keen on playing all year round or on moving his family to London, although he did want to return to rugby union. Newcastle's offer to play union only and move to the North-East seemed very attractive and when he made his first visit to Kingston Park on Sunday 29 December, that attraction turned into real enthusiasm.

Six weeks later Tuigamala was a fully-fledged Falcon and said 'I am very excited at joining Newcastle and very happy with the challenge of helping the Falcons into Division One next season. It is a challenge and a pleasure to get back to Rugby Union, although I have enjoyed my time playing League with Wigan. I am determined to make the most of it and make a big impact on Newcastle who are an ambitious club, determined to go forward, and that is what attracted me to them'. The respect between the club and its new signing was mutual as Rob Andrew hailed Tuigamala as 'a class act off the field as well as on it. You get a chance to sign a truly world class player like Inga once in a lifetime and we are delighted to have him at Kingston Park. He is a massively important piece in the professional jigsaw we are putting together at Newcastle. Having one of the biggest names in world rugby playing at Newcastle would have been unthinkable twelve months ago. Now it is reality. The signing also underlines the bigger picture at Kingston Park, which shows how the board views rugby and where the game is heading. They have shown they are prepared to invest to increase the interest level of spectators, television and press. That is why everyone in the North East is now talking about rugby…Inga is a magnificent ambassador for rugby, himself and now for Newcastle…we have some guys who have already become cult figures at Kingston Park. Inga will become the cult of all cults. He will become a hero in the dressing room as well as on the terraces and his influence on the younger players will be enormous. Personally I have been a fan of Inga's throughout his career, particularly after he ran all over me when I was playing for the British Lions in the Second Test in 1993 and never even broke stride to see if I was all right! He is one of the world's leading rugby stars of either code.'

Tuigamala's reputation as a rugby player is immense. He played 39 times for New Zealand before opting to play for his native Samoa after a spell of great success in Rugby League. He did express some regrets about leaving League and Wigan but revealed that it had always been his intention to return to his roots. Since joining Wigan in January 1994, Tuigamala had won two Challenge Cup winners medals, two Regal Trophy winners medals and a Premiership winner's medal.

It was Tuigamala who insisted at the start of the following season that the Falcons would win the Premiership, a forecast that prompted much scoffing by one local rugby journalist from whom Tuigamala extracted a promise he would shave his head if Newcastle did win the title and said journalist (yours truly) paid the price at Harlequins nine months later. Tuigamala's almost evangelical zeal for rugby and his Christian beliefs makes him an ideal role-model for youngsters and since his arrival at Kingston Park he has been the most sought after player for autograph hunters, sponsors and fans and he rarely fails them

Tuigamala's arrival was greeted with glee by the rest of the Newcastle squad, and for Pat Lam it was reunion time as the two had played together since the age of sixteen in Auckland and Lam was captain when Tuigamala appeared in the Test for Samoa against Ireland. 'It will be good to have another brother in this part of the world' said Lam, 'We came through the grades together in New Zealand and we're still great friends. I've seen a huge change in him since he went through a rough patch with the selectors in the early 1990s. He is a complete gentleman and a total rugby player.'

However, all was not sweetness and light over the signing. Newcastle came in for a fair amount of criticism from leading figures in the game accusing the club and Sir John Hall of playing over the odds for players and inflating the burgeoning transfer market. The Newcastle chairman refuted the criticism in his usual forthright manner, declaring that 'We aim to compete with the best and the signing of Tuigamala shows we mean business. We're also in the market place and that's where the players are. There are other owner-investors in the game and we want to be the best. Each owner-investor will decide how much he is prepared to pay…that's the market place. We have got to invest in the sport and we have probably invested more in rugby this year than the RFU have in the last 100 years.'

Perhaps the euphoria of Tuigamala's signing should have been enough to carry Newcastle through to the Pilkington Cup semi-final but they suffered a hugely deflating defeat by Leicester 18-8 in the quarter-final at Kingston Park with six penalties from the boot of South African Joel Stransky and a masterful display from England flanker Neil Back – who made it his personal business to get up Rob Andrew's nose throughout the match and the Newcastle player manager was given scant protection by his colleagues who seemed to suffer from stage fright. Ironically, it was Newcastle skipper Dean Ryan who came in for criticism from Leicester manager Bob Dwyer. The former Wallaby World Cup coach accused Ryan of taking 'cheap shots' by throwing punches when he didn't have to. Ryan's reaction was typically combative: 'I make no apology for the way I play,' said Ryan; 'I play a physically committed

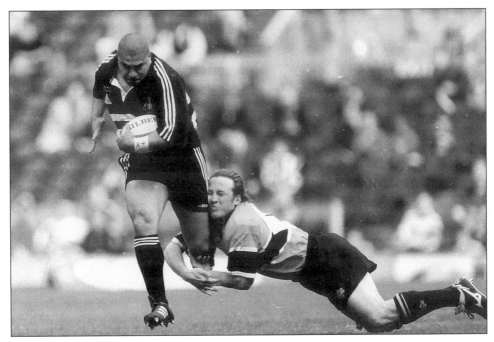

Inga Tuigamala followed Pat Lam to Newcastle and his power and pace were also key factors in Newcastle's promotion drive and Premiership success.

game and I don't feel I have anything to apologise for. Bob Dwyer should put up or shut up. If he's got a complaint he should make it through official channels.' There is, of course, a delightful sequel to the confrontation with Dwyer and Ryan becoming manager and coach of rejuvenated Bristol in 1999 with their past differences seemingly forgotten (although Dwyer has since moved on and Ryan has assumed full control at the Memorial Ground).

An extremely eventful February 1997 closed with Alan Tait being called up for Scotland and in doing so becoming the first player to play Rugby Union for Scotland having played Rugby League, thereby demolishing another of the barriers between the two codes. With the unerring capacity that Tait has for the dramatic, he scored the first of Scotland's five tries in a 38-10 demolition of Ireland at Murrayfield.

Va'aiga Tuigamala's debut the following month in a 57-10 win over Wakefield was watched by a crowd of 3,700, but John Bentley stole the big man's thunder by scoring four tries to give his British Lions selection hopes a major boost. The crowd did not like it much when Tuigamala gave Bentley the scoring pass for his fourth try as they wanted to see Tuigamala score himself! It was a win Newcastle needed after the postponement of games because of international call-ups and they were down in fourth place in Division Two, nine points adrift of leaders Richmond and five behind second placed Bedford, but with four and five games in hand respectively. It was to lead to a frantic end-of-season charge for the Falcons as they chased promotion.

10
FALCONS BECOME LIONS

International call-ups were becoming the norm for the Falcons but Jack Rowell's call to Rob Andrew on 12 March 1997 was a real surprise. Rowell wanted another Newcastle player to join his squad as cover for Mike Catt, who'd been promoted to the side to face Wales in Cardiff following a hip injury to Paul Grayson, and the Falcons player he wanted was Andrew himself.

Andrew had called it quits on his international career when he parted company with Wasps for Newcastle but he was happy to respond to Rowell's request and, at the age of thirty-four, he came off the bench for Catt with eight minutes of the game left for his 71st and final England cap as England hammered Wales 34-13. After years of being a member of England side who underachieved against the Welsh, especially in Cardiff, Andrew found his swansong somewhat emotional as it was his last match and also the last international at the Arms Park before the stadium was torn down to be rebuilt as The Millennium Stadium for the 1999 World Cup.

It was back to business the next day for the Newcastle manager with half the Falcons dashing back from international duty, Doddie Weir, Alan Tait, Peter Walton and Gary Armstrong flying back from the France *v.* Scotland game and Andrew, Tim Stimpson and Tony Underwood driving back from Cardiff for their Division Two game against Nottingham at Kingston Park.

Newcastle won 53-17 despite Tait and Walton being ruled out with injuries from the day before and Andrew admitted he'd got away with gambling on playing the match the day after the international doubleheader. It was the final round of the Five Nations Championship which was something of a relief for the Newcastle players who were able to turn their attention fully to winning promotion, although there was the inevitable added pressure of the announcement of the British Lions tour squad to South Africa yet to come. Doddie Weir meanwhile became the proud possessor of the Falcons' first national trophy when he was voted The Famous Grouse Scotland Player of the Five Nations Championship – Alan Tait was named runner-up.

Newcastle followed up victory over Nottingham with a devastating 88-19 win over Moseley. There was another John Bentley hat trick and, despite the challenge of Coventry and Bedford, only one team really stood between Newcastle and promotion to the top flight. That team was Richmond and their challenge was summarily dismissed 37-17 at Kingston Park in front of a record crowd of 5,700.

There was more reason for celebration at Kingston Park three days later when manager Fran Cotton and coach Ian McGeechan announced their British Lions squad of thirty-five for South Africa and it included Falcons Doddie Weir, Tony Underwood, Tim Stimpson, Alan Tait and John Bentley – Underwood's selection was perhaps the most remarkable as he had forced his way in after being omitted from the preliminary party of the sixty-two.

Rob Andrew in contemplative mood after being recalled to the England side to face Wales by Jack Rowell.

Weir said he would be celebrating with a 'wee nip of malt' and Stimpson could hardly contain his excitement after a momentous twelve months which had seen him start as an England A player, progress to the Five Nations Championship and finish as a British Lion. Manager Rob Andrew described the news as just reward for the players who had worked very hard all season, stating 'We've always set out to build a side which will go places not to just survive at the top level but one which can compete and we looked for the right individuals and it's paid off for the club and for the players.'

There was only one discordant note with Newcastle chairman Sir John Hall fearing his players were being subjected to too much rugby. 'Naturally, I'm delighted for the players' said Sir John, 'but I am very concerned as chairman of the club about players being asked to play too much. I have to ask the question if they are going to be worn out for the start of what could be a very important season for us in 1997/98. I do realise what it means to the players but if Newcastle were to fade in the second half of the season because the players are worn out and we missed out on winning something, I don't think the club, the fans or myself would be too pleased. I know the British Lions means a lot to the players but everybody says the players are playing too many games and I'd really like them to have a break, a rest and holiday with their families and ideally they should have two months off. I recognise the honour for the players but they are full-time professionals and we are paying their wages.'

In the run-up to Newcastle's next game, manager Rob Andrew spoke about the need for his players to re-focus after their win against Richmond and the hullabaloo of the Lions selection and he must have sensed what was coming because the Falcons lost 34-28 at Bedford – a club they have always had problems playing against. It was Newcastle's second league defeat of the season and the absence of skipper Dean Ryan with injury was a crucial

Newcastle's five British Lions, 1997: John Bentley, Tim Stimpson, Doddie Weir, Alan Tait and Tony Underwood.

factor, as was the fractured jaw suffered by Tony Underwood in very physical match with yellow cards being shown to Bedford's Steve McCurrie and Junior Paramore for high tackles and Newcastle's Ireland and British Lions prop Nick Popplewell for punching Bedford second row Scott Murray, who had to go to hospital with a nasty eye injury.

No-one can condone what Popplewell did and he should have been shown the red card but referee Steve Lander, acting on the advice of his touch judge who, like many others had seen Murray sweep Doddie Weir's legs from under him in the line-out and Popplewell throw the punch as a result Murray's illegal challenge, advocated a yellow card. That should have been the end of the affair with even Murray admitting he'd got what he deserved but the Newcastle prop was subjected to an unpalatable trial by television with Sky and BBC's *Rugby Special* showing the punch several times in slow motion and almost demanding disciplinary action. Unfortunately, the television critics failed to include the tackle which led to Underwood's broken jaw and the high tackles by McCurrie and Paramore in their sweeping condemnation and Newcastle's players and management were left with a sense of injustice that Popplewell had been singled out. It didn't help when RFU secretary Tony Hallett urged Newcastle to take action against Popplewell and Frank Warren, then owner of Bedford, joined in the clamour for Popplewell's head.

Newcastle reprimanded Popplewell and fined him £1,000 which failed to satisfy Bedford or the RFU whose disciplinary officer Roy Manock decided that Popplewell should face a tribunal, where he was handed a thirty day ban which ruled him out of Newcastle's final two league games and the first week of the following season.

11
PROMOTION

Newcastle refused to let the Popplewell incident affect them or to worry about a growing list of injuries as the promotion chase entered the final phase and wins against Coventry 49-17, Blackheath 72-10 and Rotherham 45-21 in the space of eight days put the Falcons back on track and within touching distance of Division One.

They needed just three points from their remaining three games to make sure of going up. Two of those points came a 71-20 win over London Scottish and Rob Andrew conceded that Newcastle were unlikely to blow it from there. They did not and a 66-24 win at Waterloo four days later followed by a 61-13 win at home to Rotherham on 4 May in front of a crowd of 4,400 saw Newcastle return to rugby's elite by finishing second in Division Two, one point behind Richmond, with a playing record from 22 games of: won 19, drawn 1, lost 2, points for 1,255, points against 346, with a total of 39 points.

Newcastle skipper Dean Ryan missed the final game after breaking an arm in the match at Waterloo and it needed an operation to pin and plate the break; he was kept in hospital overnight but he was back on his feet and watching from the sidelines on 4 May. 'It's been a hard season,' said manager Rob Andrew, 'and playing in Division One will be a tremendous challenge. It won't be easy and a lot will depend on how quickly we adjust to the pace of first division rugby, week-in, week-out. I think we have players who can play at First Division level but we will have a big game every weekend not just once in a while and we have to get used to that.' Andrew also made it clear he would be looking at strengthening his squad and altering the balance between professional and semi-professional more towards the former, but pointed out that the market had changed and that players were now more costly and a transfer fee would be involved unless the player came from abroad or was a free agent.

Chairman Sir John Hall revelled in the prospect of the Falcons challenging for the First Division title and the European Cup – he was to become a very happy man the following season when Newcastle realised his dream of the Premiership but was then disappointed when the English clubs' boycott of the European Cup cost the Falcons dearly by denying them their chance to compete as English champions – but for the moment he was able to savour promotion. 'It's what we planned for,' he said, 'and it's great for the club and the fans. Our target now is to get a team together to win the league and to go on and win in Europe.' So, it was mission accomplished and while Newcastle did not win the Division Two Championship they were back among the elite of English club rugby and would be competing the new Premiership Division One the next season, Allied Dunbar having taken over the sponsorship of the leagues from Courage.

There was precious little rest for Newcastle's big names as they linked up with the British Lions party and the fractured jaw suffered by Underwood in the Bedford game threatened his tour hopes. Fortunately it was not a serious break and he recovered in time to play a full part in the tour, where he was joint top try scorer along with John Bentley.

Job well done. Inga Tuigamala congratulates Rob Andrew on clinching promotion to Division One at Rotherham.

Rob Andrew acknowledges the Falcons' travelling support at Rotherham after Newcastle ensured a return to the top flight.

Bentley also had his problems before being able to join the party for South Africa because of a contractual dispute with Halifax Blue Sox, who demanded compensation for his absence as he was due to return to them during the summer and play Super League. Bentley made it clear there was no way he would not be on the plane to South Africa and the matter was eventually resolved by Bentley agreeing to play a number of extra games for the Blue Sox to see out his contract.

The disappointment felt by Newcastle lock Garath Archer in not being among those who would fly out to the Republic was assuaged somewhat when he was named in the England party for their summer tour to Argentina, but his hopes were dashed again when he had to withdraw because of a damaged disc in his neck, while Peter Walton and George Graham were also selected for Scotland's tour to South Africa and Ross Nesdale for Ireland's tour to New Zealand. England Under 21s also went on tour to Australia and took Newcastle understudy hooker Ritchie Horton and centres Andy Blyth and Martin Shaw with them.

The Lions tour proved to be a success for four of the five Falcons, Doddie Weir's tour being cut short by one of the worst acts of thuggery seen on a rugby field. Weir was viciously kicked by Mpumalanga second row Marius Bosman in the Lions 64-14 win at Witbank. The act was captured on television and Bosman was later fined a paltry £1,500 for inflicting what was a career-threatening injury. Weir had to fly home and did take legal advice with a view to suing Bosman had his career been ended. Fortunately, that wasn't the case but it consigned Weir to a long period of rehabilitation and he made sure he would never forget the South African by naming the boot-scraper outside his front door 'Bosman' (which

Garath Archer was frustrated when he missed out on both the British Lions tour to South Africa and then the England tour to Argentina because of a neck problem.

means of course that every day he gets to wipe his feet on his assailant). Lions manager Fran Cotton didn't mince words when he described the incident as 'a disgraceful act of gratuitous violence that I'd thought had gone out of international rugby.'

Tim Stimpson and Tony Underwood both played in the final Test while Alan Tait and John Bentley became integral parts of the Lions' success but not after a disappointing start for Bentley, who established his claims early for a Test place with a spectacular try against Gauteng Falcons. He missed out to club colleague Tait in the first Test in Cape Town, Fran Cotton and coach Ian McGeechan springing a major surprise by selecting the Newcastle centre on the wing instead of Bentley, who was bitterly disappointed at being overlooked, as were Stimpson and Underwood.

Tait justified his selection with the crucial clinching try in the Lions 25-16 win but Bentley's hat-trick against Free State pushed him into contention for the Second Test and when Ieuan Evans tour ended with injury, Bentley joined Tait in the Lions side for Durban where the Lions won in dramatic style 18-15 thanks to Jeremy Guscott's drop goal five minutes from time – and five penalties from the boot of Neil Jenkins. A 2-0 winning lead in the series made the Lions as famous as their 1974 predecessors who also won a series in South Africa and Tait, an ardent fan of the 1970s, persuaded his team-mates to wear their shirts open-necked, the collars laid over their blazers, as a tribute to the '74 Lions on a wild night of celebration which ended with John Bentley addressing the people on Durban beachfront early in the morning from his hotel window, bellowing 'Lions 2 South Africa 0'.

Newcastle may have won promotion but they were planning for the future with their academy as well as cherry-picking some of the country's top young players. All six young guns in this picture were to play for the Falcons first team, although they would all eventually move on to other clubs. From left to right: Stuart Legg, Chris Simpson-Daniel, David Barnes, Ritchie Horton, Martin Shaw, Jim Naylor.

All that was needed to round off the tour was Test caps for Underwood and Stimpson and a 3-0 whitewash of South Africa. The first dream was realised with Underwood's selection for the starting line-up in Johannesburg and Stimpson's appearance as a first half substitute for the Newcastle wing who suffered a hip injury, but the second dream was not to be with the Lions going down 35-16. What should have happened then was the Lions returning home in triumph as the team they had become, but the England players in the Lions squad, including Bentley, Stimpson and Underwood, had to fly to Australia to link up with the main body of the England squad for a Test match against the Wallabies in Sydney…it was a prime example of the appalling planning which rugby regularly inflicts on itself.

Meanwhile, Newcastle manager Rob Andrew hadn't been just sitting around watching the Lions' progress. In a busy close season, he concentrated on signing young players in England A wing Jim Naylor from Orrell, West Hartlepool's England Under 21 prop David Barnes and full back Stuart Legg, plus a certain Jonny Wilkinson who had just played for England Schools the previous season. Andrew was also busy working with rugby development manager Paul MacKinnon to establish the club's junior academy as part of the youth set-up while Falcons skipper Dean Ryan, who was back in full training after breaking an arm in the Falcons' penultimate promotion match. Coach Steve Bates flew to New Zealand to check on the possible new signings and there were the inevitable changes as players moved on.

12
BACK IN THE BIG TIME

The Premiership and the European Conference Cup – in which they would face French sides Perpignan and Biarritz plus Edinburgh in the pool games and Castres and Agen in the knock-out stages – would pose different problems for the Falcons from those faced in the Second Division. The Falcons had been expected to win in Division Two; in Division One, they would not and manager Rob Andrew decided to take his squad on a pre-season training trip to Montflanquin in France with a game against Agen to prepare for the new campaign.

Although they would be missing big names Inga Tuigamala and John Bentley, because of a long-standing family commitment and Bentley having to fulfil his Super League obligations with Halifax Blue Sox, some good news was that Doddie Weir's recovery from his knee injury was going well and he was in with a chance of playing in the opening game of the season at Bath – a real baptism of fire for the First Division new boys. Weir made the trip to France and was able to train for the first time since Bosman had brutally ended his Lions tour. The training week was a major success and the Falcons rounded it off with an excellent 13-9 win against an Agen side that contained French skipper Abdelatif Benazzi.

While the development of the side on the field had proved more than satisfactory, the same could not be said of Newcastle's hopes of improving Kingston Park. Club officials recognised that it was an inadequate venue for First Division rugby with a capacity of only around 6,600, little covered seating (or standing for that matter), poor toilet facilities and a lack of car parking, bars and catering. With the main clubhouse almost invariably given over to corporate hospitality, there was virtually nowhere for the casual supporter to get a drink or something to eat. Plans for a covered temporary stand and additional car parking did not meet with Newcastle City council approval and were deferred which prompted Newcastle to look at alternative grounds, including Gateshead Stadium and St James's Park.

There were also rumours of the Halls selling up their stake in Newcastle United following the retirement of Sir John Hall and son Douglas Hall taking over control at St James's. It was a rumour denied by Sir John who was in France with the Falcons. 'We have no intention of pulling out of Newcastle United or the Falcons,' said Sir John. 'Why should we pull out of something we have spent a lot of time and money building up. I'm not involved in the day-to-day running of things any more but that's common knowledge and has been for a while and as far as I'm concerned our commitment to Newcastle United and the Sporting Club remains as strong as ever'. In fact, Sir John seemed to revel in the company of the Falcons and had a particular affection for Doddie Weir and Gary Armstrong, who were not above pulling Sir John's leg, something which appealed to him greatly. There seemed to be no reason why Newcastle Falcons should worry about their backers but in the long-term, Sir John's and Newcastle United's initial ardour with rugby eventually would cool and prompt a crisis which the Falcons were fortunate to survive. Ironically, what was to be one of the most momentous seasons in Newcastle's history opened with not so much a bang but a whimper on 17 August 1997 when they lost their 'friendly' against West Hartlepool 18-17 at Brierton Lane. It was an awful match with nearly 50 penalties and free-kicks awarded by referee Tony Fisher and which both former All Black Mike Brewer, West's new player-coach, and Newcastle manager Rob Andrew described as a complete waste of an afternoon. A week later, it was a different story as Newcastle shocked the established order by having the temerity to win 20-13 at Bath, championship runners-up the previous season.

The new kids on the block were as brash as ever and intent on matching any physical challenge thrown their way. Nathan Thomas was sent off after trampling on Tim Stimpson, although that was only after he had recovered from the almighty thump that Dean Ryan delivered in retribution. Ryan was shown the yellow card and it was to spark a long-running controversy that saw the intervention of RFU supremo Cliff Brittle and a ban for Ryan. Bath prop Dave Hilton and Falcons prop Paul Van-Zandvliet were also yellow carded in what was not a dirty match by any stretch of the imagination. In fact, it was a great advert for Premiership rugby with both sides playing on the edge; some of the hits were frightening and had the 8,000 capacity crowd wincing as the tackles went in. It was 13-13 after Inga Tuigamala scored a try thanks to Alan Tait's ability to see the gap and Stuart Legg, who came on as a replacement for the injured Tony Underwood, scored the winning try right at the death. The appearance of Legg was significant in respect of both Underwood and Tim Stimpson. Underwood's injury was the start of a long battle against problems with both knees and eventually he would be forced to retire from the game while Legg would become nearly an ever-present in the Falcons line-up, moving to full-back and keeping Stimpson on the sidelines to such an extent that the England full-back felt marginalized. By the end of the season, Stimpson was playing no part in the Falcons' Premiership-winning campaign and left the Kingston Park club the minute his contract ended to sign for Leicester Tigers. Underwood was sidelined for five weeks and there were fears he would need an operation on his left knee.

The bookies immediately installed Newcastle at 10-1 for the Premiership and Inga Tuigamala insisted: 'We're going to win the championship and I base my prediction purely on attitude and this team has a phenomenal attitude.' He was right and Newcastle rampaged through the European Conference games after their first home Premiership game against Northampton was postponed because of the tragic death of Diana, Princess of Wales, in a car crash in Paris.

The Conference proved an ideal vehicle for the Falcons to get their act together and they got into the winning habit in the pool games by beating Biarritz 37-10, Perpignan 60-3 and 27-13, Edinburgh 40-16 and 72-24, but came a cropper at Biarritz 32-28, which was to cost them dearly because it meant they would then be away in the semi-finals at Agen after they'd beaten Castres 44-0 in the quarter-finals – and Agen, having learned their lesson from the pre-season defeat, were waiting for them, squeezing the life out of the Falcons back line on their way to 12-9 win.

The Falcons' win at Perpignan was an interesting experience for some of the younger players with a volatile crowd off the pitch and an equally volatile Perpignan side on it. Cushions, oranges, coins and cans of beer were among the missiles that zipped through the night air when the players came close to the touchline and it is just as well the crowd were fenced in. Falcons skipper Dean Ryan was felled by a punch from behind late in the game, which was

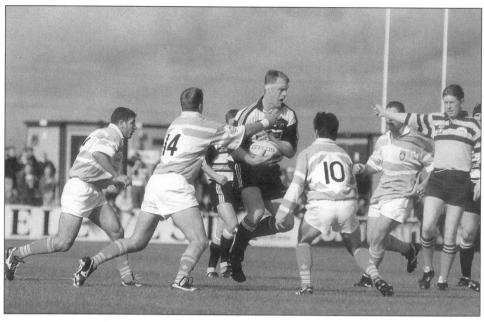

Richard Arnold in the thick of the action during Newcastle's European Conference game against Perpignan. He looks like he's taking on the French side on his own!

Richard Arnold drives on against Perpignan.

punctuated by several fights, and on the final whistle the Falcons players shot off the pitch and into the changing room led by player-manager Rob Andrew, whose experience of playing in France for a year with Toulouse had obviously taught him not to hang about in those circumstances.

Despite the disappointment of the semi-final defeat in Agen, which was a distraction from the Premiership the Falcons could have done without in late December, the European Conference was seen by the Falcons management as a very useful exercise and the pool games as good grounding for their return to Premiership action against Northampton.

It seemed they might have to do that without skipper Dean Ryan when he was handed a shock twenty-eight day ban for the punch he'd thrown to fell Nathan Thomas in the opening Premiership game against Bath. Ryan was banned more than six weeks after the game at a disciplinary panel held at Darlington on the insistence of RFU management committee chairman Cliff Brittle, who had watched the Bath *v.* Newcastle game on television and wrote to RFU disciplinary officer Roy Manock insisting that Ryan was charged, like Nick Popplewell had been the previous season, with 'conduct prejudicial to the interests of the game'. Newcastle appealed. They were furious with the sentence and made it clear they would pursue the case all the way to court if they had to. Ryan's sentence was ultimately halved to fourteen days by Judge Baker when the case went to independent arbitration and he missed no Premiership matches at all. It all smacked of an exercise in futility and not for the first time had rugby and the RFU appeared to shoot itself in the foot. Certainly the initial ban and the need to appeal was not the sort of problem Newcastle wanted as they turned their attention back to the Premiership and visit of Northampton.

All the fuss did not affect Ryan, who played in the match and was immense as Newcastle went to the top of the table with a five-try 37-12 hammering of the Saints, a win watched by England coach Clive Woodward. The manner of victory sent a clear message to the rest of the Premiership that Newcastle were not just there to make up the numbers and love him or hate him – and Newcastle fans loved Ryan's uncompromising, winning attitude while referees did not – you could not keep the big Falcons skipper out of the limelight, the action or the headlines.

The introduction of the sin-bin, two months after the start of the season, was a case in point. There seemed a certain inevitability that Ryan would be the first player to experience the ten minute cooler and he didn't disappoint when he was shown the white card (it was eventually changed to yellow in subsequent seasons) in Newcastle's 35-19 win at London Irish by referee Doug Chapman, who cornered his own little bit of history as did Ryan by becoming the first English player sin-binned in the league.

The Newcastle skipper couldn't have cared less that he went into the record books as the first English player to be sin-binned in a domestic competition, because Newcastle looked like becoming the first club to follow winning promotion by going straight on to collect the First Division title, especially as the London Irish win followed a difficult match at Sale which the Falcons won 33-26 with a late charge to victory, and an 18-12 win at home to Richmond with Andrew kicking six penalties in a forgettable match in terms of quality.

In between those two Premiership wins there was the hiccup of defeat at Biarritz in the European Conference where the Falcons managed to throw away a 25-9 lead and lose 32-28. The defeat did have serious consequences as it seemed to lead to differences between British

Newcastle's European Conference games proved costly for both John Bentley and Tim Stimpson as they lost their places in the Newcastle team after the defeat in Biarritz and never really got back into contention. Stimpson moved on to Leicester at the end of the season and Bentley went back to Rugby League club Halifax Blue Sox.

Two great Newcastle number tens together. Rob Andrew discusses the finer points of fly-half play with David Johnson, who played for Gosforth and Newcastle Gosforth with distinction.

Just one more please Rob. Don't worry – he did sign it!

Lions John Bentley and Tim Stimpson and the Falcons management. Both were left out of the side for the next Premiership game at Sale. It was the beginning of the end at Newcastle for both players, and there were rumours that both Stimpson and Bentley were unhappy with the forward-orientated style of the Falcons play and had had frank discussions with Andrew, Ryan and Bates…and there would be only be one winner in that argument!

Both men were still missing from the Newcastle side that beat Richmond and following Newcastle's win at London Irish, Stimpson found himself placed on the transfer list after discussions over a new contract did not go well. Stimpson made only three more appearances for Newcastle that season as he was forced to sit it out until the end of his contract with most clubs put off by Newcastle's asking price (believed to be a transfer fee of £200,000). It was a real waste of a talented player but also a salutary lesson from the Falcons management that they would manage things their way. It would not be the last time Andrew would display the uncompromising, ruthless streak he has and which makes him a winner. Stimpson left the club within days of the end of the season as a free agent and signed for Leicester, but he has no doubt the period he spent on the sidelines with Newcastle stalled his career. Bentley, who also made just four more appearances, one as substitute, for Newcastle after the Biarritz debacle, returned to Halifax Blue Sox during the summer and his contract with the Falcons was not renewed the following season.

A win over Gloucester 37-27 was followed by that 12-9 European Conference Shield semi-final defeat at Agen, but Bristol were hammered 50-8 to see Newcastle back on top of the Premiership and it was dawning on the rest of the country that the Falcons would take some shifting – especially when they did what clubs aren't expected to do and won at Welford Road.

13
CHAMPIONS

Newcastle's 25-19 victory over Leicester at Welford Road was another watershed for the Falcons players. They started to believe they could really win the title, although the victory in a pulsating match did little to silence the critics.

Pat Lam was simply superb, scoring two tries as the Falcons pack more than matched the Tigers' forwards in front of a 16,000 capacity crowd, but Tigers boss Bob Dwyer could not resist having a swipe after the match and the following weekend in the *Sunday Times* accusing Newcastle of pushing the laws (rules) to the limit and being 'big on gamesmanship and extremely streetwise'. Newcastle manager Rob Andrew refused to get involved in a slanging match but he, and the rest of the Falcons, were privately overjoyed to hear an Australian having a good whinge.

The match was played the night before New Year's Eve and just three days after the emphatic win over Bristol – another example of rugby's apparently intractable chaotic fixture arrangements. It seemed nothing could stop Newcastle and it looked as if the Falcons did not need British Lions wing John Bentley, with Jim Naylor proving a more than able replacement as he ran in a hat-trick of tries in the 46-13 win over London Irish.

Newcastle then announced plans to play their Premiership match against Bath at Gateshead International Stadium. It was an immense risk both in terms of spectator interest and also surrendering their Kingston Park fortress – where they had not lost in the league since 6 January 1996 – to play against the country's most dangerous side thirsting for revenge for that opening day defeat at The Recreation Ground. It was a bold gamble, but problems with persuading Newcastle City Council to allow development of Kingston Park and the difficulties of handling big crowds with limited facilities prompted the Falcons to have talks with Gateshead Stadium and Gateshead Council (who were only too happy to see the North-East's top club playing South of the Tyne). The same could not be said of the Newcastle fans and the club could have ended up with egg on their faces. In the event they were delighted when all 11,000 tickets for the game were sold. 'The decision to move the game was a difficult one because we do enjoy playing at Kingston Park,' said Rob Andrew, 'but the fact is that in order to take the club forward off the field and match what we are doing on it we have to continue the search for better facilities for the North-East public who want to watch top-class rugby.' In the event, the North-East weather put paid to what would have the biggest crowd to watch a Premiership game on Tyneside. Torrential rain left the Gateshead pitch waterlogged and the game was called off some three and half hours before kick-off.

It was a bitter disappointment for Newcastle, not just in terms of having sold so many tickets, but because the games were piling up and four big matches were facing re-arrangement – Bath, Saracens and Wasps (twice) because of postponements caused by European and Tetley's Bitter Cup ties and the weather. Selling so many tickets did raise

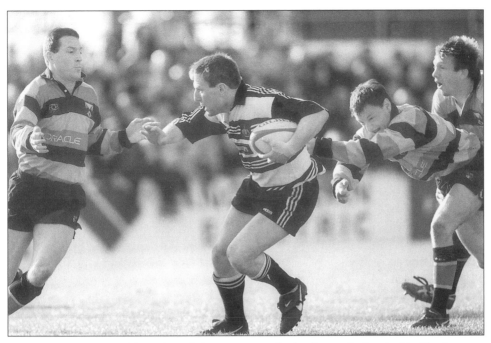

Gary Armstrong surrounded by Richmond players as Newcastle edge closer to the Premiership title. Armstrong wasn't on the score sheet at Kingston Park in October but his half-back partner Rob Andrew was with six penalties in an 18-12 win.

Rob Andrew in typically aggressive mode as Newcastle continue their drive for the Premiership title against Bath.

the possibility of St James's Park being used for the Falcons four end-of-season matches and Andrew had discussions with Sir John Hall, before the idea was vetoed because of fears that the rugby players would damage the St James's pitch.

With Newcastle on course for a Premiership and Tetley's Bitter Cup double, the Falcons were expected to roll over Worcester and move into the Cup quarter-finals without too much trouble, but Les Cusworth's side made them fight all the way and Newcastle were relieved to get away from Sixways with a 10-0 victory. They were drawn away to Northampton in the next round where they disappointingly made their exit 17-7 – although it was almost inevitable as the Falcons had won at Franklins Gardens 21-17 just four weeks before the quarter-finals in a controversial Premiership match with the Saints claiming they'd 'scored' two tries which weren't given and should have also been awarded a penalty try.

In between Newcastle's return to Franklins Gardens for the cup tie, they crushed Harlequins 43-15 and England coach Clive Woodward called up eighteen year old Jonny Wilkinson for training with the full England squad although he had only played four games for the Falcons. Wilkinson's performances with England Under 21s had been phenomenal but Newcastle were adamant they would not rush him into situations he could not yet handle. However, Wilkinson did make his Premiership debut for Newcastle shortly afterwards in the home game against Saracens on 25 March and came on a substitute for England in the Five Nations Championship game with Ireland at Twickenham on 4 April – the roar from the 75,000 capacity crowd signalling the start of what looks certain to be a long and illustrious international career.

Defeat in the Tetley's Bitter Cup at Northampton 17-7 was a setback for Newcastle in terms of confidence and meant they were out of another competition they believed they'd win. A capacity crowd of 8,000 were then treated to one of the great games in a season of great games. There was an inevitable hangover from the Cup defeat and after racing into a 17-0 lead in their next Premiership game, Newcastle lost the plot and were forced to hang on desperately as Sale came back at them and were lucky to hang on to their unbeaten league record with a narrow 23-18 triumph.

The Falcons' fantastic league form was bringing them continual recognition on the national stage with Jonny Wilkinson, Tony Underwood, Garath Archer and Dean Ryan called up for the England squad for the game against Scotland (although only Ryan and Archer played in the game with Underwood pulling out through injury and Wilkinson being judged not yet ready for the Five Nations Championship cauldron). Ryan was back in the England squad at the age of thirty-one, four years after his last appearance and even if he was to be left out after playing against Scotland it was a justified selection and Ryan was worth his fourth cap.

The recognition was all very nice, but distracting and it increased the pressure on the Falcons squad. It was beginning to show, especially when Newcastle lost their first Premiership game of the season going down 30-17 at Richmond, which left them two points adrift of leaders Saracens. With two games in hand on the London club, there was no real reason for panic but, having gone out of the European Conference Cup in the semi-finals, the Tetley's Bitter Cup in the quarter-finals and now having lost their unbeaten Premiership record, there was a nagging fear the Falcons could end the season with nothing, not even a place in the European Cup with the English clubs having decided to boycott the competition in a row over money and representation rights.

It made the clash with Saracens at Kingston Park on 25 March a real crunch game and it was a significant win for the Falcons for three reasons. The first was that the 30-25 scoreline took Newcastle to the top of the table on points difference. The second was a full Premiership debut for Jonny Wilkinson and the third was the news that Newcastle were considering a move to Gateshead International Stadium to play all their home games there the following season. Just over 7,000 spectators were shoe-horned into Kingston Park for the win over Saracens and Newcastle were still actively looking at alternative sites and ideas after running into many obstacles to improving capacity and facilities at Kingston Park. One of them was the possibility of building a 10,000 all-seater stadium alongside Gateshead Stadium while playing matches there in the meantime and they had also checked on sites in Shieldfield and Walkergate on the outskirts of the city.

'We have looked at a number of sites and there are a number of options,' said Ken Nottage, Newcastle Sporting Club's chief executive, 'but there has been no decision yet'. Newcastle did go ahead with their plans to play at Gateshead but abandoned the experiment after only four games because of disappointing attendances and returned to Kingston Park.

The win over Saracens was vital for the confidence of the players, especially as they faced another big game at home to Wasps and it was yet another bruising encounter. Despite what both clubs have said and will, no doubt, say again in the future, there is certainly a depth of feeling in Newcastle v. Wasps games because of the history between the two clubs. Newcastle edged home 20-13 after Andrew had scored a rare try in the third minute, with Stuart Legg adding a second just before half time. With Andrew belting over a penalty and conversion, Newcastle looked to be cruising at 20-3 before Wasps, the champions, showed remarkable powers of recovery to claw their way back to 20-13 and it needed a last-gasp crunching tackle from Tony Underwood to prevent a score and the possibility of a draw.

It didn't get any easier with Gloucester at Kingsholm next up. A 12,000 packed house saw the Falcons ride their luck and win 29-27 to get one hand on the Premiership trophy as they led the table by two points from Saracens with a game in hand. The Kingsholm crowd were baying for Durham referee John Pearson's blood by the end of a controversial match. Pearson gave three crucial decisions which were replayed on a giant screen and which sent the Gloucester crowd into a paroxysm of near hysteria. It mattered not that Pearson was later proved right in two of his three decisions and that he could not be blamed for the third because he did not have a clear view of what happened. All the crowd cared about was that their side had been denied. Pearson awarded a penalty try with Newcastle 13-3 down after Gloucester dropped the scrum and for the second match running Andrew scored a crucial try that gave Falcons a 17-13 lead. Amazingly, Andrew grabbed a second try to make it 24-21. It was soon 24-24 and when Dean Ryan collared Scott Benton at a line-out, he looked offside. The crowd thought so, the touch judge thought so, Pearson did not (and he was right as the video was to prove later). The result was a try from Peter Walton and if the uproar that followed was deafening it was nothing compared with the volcanic explosion that followed Paul Van-Zandvliet's bodycheck-cum-trip on Mark Mapletoft as he chipped ahead.

Mapletoft went flying in a swan-dive that was worth 5.9 for technical merit and 6.0 for artistic interpretation. There was only one problem, referee Pearson was looking the other way at the ball which was being collected by Gary Armstrong although he caught a glimpse from the corner of his eye and he knew something had happened. He awarded a penalty on the basis of that and it led to calls for a penalty try although Gloucester's director of rugby Richard Hill agreed with Pearson and most neutral observers that a penalty was the right decision. It was a crucial moment in a crucial passage of play as Newcastle hung on, despite a Mapletoft penalty to cut their lead to 29-27 and a drop goal shot from the fly half which drifted just wide in the closing seconds.

If that was heart-stopping, it was nothing compared with the three matches in eight days the Falcons now embarked on and which was to decide whether they would be champions or not; for a brief period it seemed they would not go on to lift the Premiership. In a season of incredibly tight matches, there would not be two closer encounters than the games at Vicarage Road and Loftus Road. Saracens fly half Michael Lynagh had good cause to remember Rob Andrew's injury-time drop goal that had sent Australia tumbling out of the World Cup in Cape Town. Three years after that quarter-final, the Wallaby ace tasted a sweet revenge when he slotted an injury-time drop goal to snatch a 12-10 win for Saracens in front of a record crowd of 19,674. 'A world-class drop goal from a world-class fly half' was how Andrew described it. 'We just looked at each other and shrugged. We didn't have to say anything. I think Michael owed me that one from 1995, but I did think we had nicked it when Pat Lam scored with ten minutes to go, but Michael and I know we both have to win our remaining games and no-one is going to let it go without a fight.'

The result left Newcastle and Saracens both on 30 points with Newcastle just top on points difference and with one game still in hand. The following Wednesday the Falcons were at Loftus Road and they lost another cracker 18-17 after leading 17-13 with twenty minutes left, a Mike Friday try sending them tumbling to their second, successive defeat as Rob Andrew missed two penalties in the last five minutes. Again, there was no love lost as Wasps second row Mark Weedon was yellow carded for thumping Andrew and Dean Ryan was cautioned by referee Ashley Rowden after getting involved in a scrap between Gary Armstrong and Buster White. Andrew's two misses, one of which he would normally kick in his sleep, left the Newcastle manager distraught, but Steve Bates was phlegmatic in his response: 'No-one blames Rob for missing the kicks. It's just ridiculous to have to play two games of this intensity in the space of four days. You just cannot ask players to perform at the top of the game with so little recovery time.'

Bates feared it would be very difficult to get the Newcastle players back up for the following Sunday's game at Bristol. It was a must-win game with Newcastle just hanging on to the top spot. Bates was right: Newcastle were pale shadow of their normal selves but they were facing the Premiership's bottom club and they knew they could move one point clear of Saracens, who had drawn 10-10 with Leicester the day before, if they won. They did win 43-18 but there was no doubt the Premiership would go right down to the wire, especially when Saracens went back to the top of the table with wins at Harlequins 28-26 and at home to London Irish 29-21.

More than 7,000 were at Gateshead Stadium to see Newcastle win 27-10 against Leicester to cut Saracens' lead to just one point. It was match riddled with controversy. England centre Will Greenwood was sent off for allegedly head-butting Rob Andrew in the final minutes. The Newcastle player-manager converted the three tries by Gary Armstrong, Pat Lam and

Peter Walton and kicked two late penalties. Once again there was controversy surrounding the match with photographs appearing to show Newcastle prop Paul Van-Zandvliet biting Leicester flanker Neil Back on the head during one of the mass brawls and off-the-ball incidents which punctuated the game. Yellow cards were shown to Leicester props Darren Garforth and Graham Rowntree and Newcastle flanker Richard Arnold, as well as the red card to Greenwood by referee Ed Morrison. Back later said 'I can't remember being bitten on the head at any stage. I was bitten on the thumb at some stage in the match but I have no complaints because, in the act of pushing a player away, my thumb could have been accidentally bitten'. Although pictures of the incident appeared graphic and damning, video evidence was viewed by both clubs, with RFU disciplinary officer Roy Manock hovering in the background again, and proved inconclusive.

It was not a good period for the North Shields-born prop as he also appeared in court charged with selling counterfeit sports goods at a local car boot sale. He pleaded not guilty and was later cleared of all charges. Neither did the incident during the Leicester game result in any disciplinary action. Leicester made no formal complaint and also decided that Greenwood should not be disciplined as they felt the clash of heads with Rob Andrew was accidental. The RFU agreed when they decided the sending off was sufficient punishment and did not ban him. They also cleared Van-Zandvliet after investigating the alleged biting incident.

The victory over Leicester left Newcastle on the verge of winning the Premiership, although Saracens were also not out of it by any stretch of the imagination and were going for the double with the Tetley's Bitter Cup final against Wasps also on their agenda. They also had one more league game against Northampton the Thursday after their Twickenham date. Saracens won with some style 48-18 at Twickenham but the Falcons took advantage of their rival's cup involvement to go top of the table with a 20-15 win over Bath at Gateshead, with 11,000 turning up in the pouring rain to watch a nervous Newcastle rely on Rob Andrew's golden boot after tries by Tony Underwood and Richard Arnold and five Jon Callard penalties for Bath. Andrew slotted two late penalties, one from 45 metres, to see Newcastle to victory in a match that went into nine minutes of injury time.

Newcastle's performance was not a good one and could be explained, to some extent, by the loss of skipper Dean Ryan after only ten minutes with a neck injury. Ryan was stretchered off after being prone on the ground for several minutes but even tried to come back on and had to be restrained by club doctor George Douglas, whom Ryan dwarfed (and who showed remarkable courage in getting in Ryan's way as he tried to get back on the pitch). Ryan was clearly concussed and missed the Falcons' final league game at Harlequins the following week.

The result put Newcastle one point ahead of Saracens and with a points difference that was 69 better than the London side's. It was clear that a draw at Harlequins would do even if Saracens defeated Northampton in their final league game in midweek. Saracens did just that with a 43-20 result after which Michael Lynagh and French international Phillipe Sella announced their retirements.

The build-up to the game at Harlequins was amazing with Newcastle gripped by a football and rugby frenzy. Newcastle United were in the FA Cup final on the Saturday

Newcastle skipper Dean Ryan is finally persuaded to leave the field after being stretchered off with a neck injury against Bath. He tried to come back on and it took the efforts of club doctor George Douglas and physiotherapist Marten Brewer to persuade him to finally leave the field. He was later diagnosed as having concussion and missed the Falcons' final match of the season at Harlequins.

against Arsenal and the Falcons were expected to bring back the Premiership from The Stoop the following day. The double would have been a fitting reward for Sir John Hall but he had to be satisfied with the Premiership title as United under-performed and lost 2-0 at Wembley, watched by the Falcons squad. There was little chance Newcastle would drift into the game on a cloud of complacency given the number of experienced players they had in their squad and the fact that Rob Andrew, Steve Bates and Dean Ryan had all been in this position before with Wasps. In fact, the players were given a real rap by Ryan, who would be on the sidelines because of concussion. 'To be frank our performance against Bath was appalling' he said on the eve of the match at The Stoop, 'and there has to be massive improvement. I'm well aware of the emotion surrounding the Premiership. That's obvious to anyone who has seen the apprehension in some of our recent performances and the evident relief when we have won but everyone has to keep a cap on those emotions because these games have a habit of jumping up and slapping you in the face.' As it turned out he needn't have worried, there was an air of expectancy amongst the Newcastle squad and they felt they had come too far to let their chance slip away now.

The only worry was that Sky Television commentator Stuart Barnes had tipped the Falcons to win comfortably. All season the Newcastle players had gathered in front of the television before their games to listen to Barnes write them off in match after match. It became something of a tradition, almost a superstition, and the players loved it when the former England and Bath fly half kept tipping the opposition to burst the Newcastle bubble. When he tipped them to win at Harlequins and win the title there was disquiet among some. Luckily he was right for once and Newcastle cruised through the game 44-20 watched by their ecstatic Toon Platoon supporters (bolstered by several recruits from the Toon Army who stayed on in London after the Cup Final. The game was watched by a crowd of 8,897 and Newcastle were 17-0 up inside twenty minutes and never in any danger of being caught. The teams who played that day were:

Harlequins: J. Williams, D. O'Leary, J. Ngauamo, P. Mensah, D. Luger, T. Lacroix, H. Harries (N. Walshe 62), J. Leonard, K. Wood (captain), A. Yates, G. Llewellyn, T. Collier, R. Jenkins, L. Cabannes, S. White-Cooper.

Newcastle: S. Legg, J. Naylor, J. Wilkinson, V. Tuigamala (A. Tait 67), T. Underwood, R. Andrew, G. Armstrong (captain), N. Popplewell (G. Graham 48), R. Nesdale (R. Horton 80), P. Van-Zandvliet, G. Archer, D. Weir (R. Metcalfe 77), P. Lam, R. Arnold (S. O'Neill 77), P. Walton.

The referee was A. Rowden (RFU).

Two tries from Gary Armstrong, plus one apiece from Pat Lam, Rob Andrew, Richard Arnold and Nick Popplewell, and four conversions and two penalties from Andrew were the bare facts of the Falcons' Premiership triumph. They played like true champions and the celebrations on the pitch afterwards with players and fans together were something to see – especially when Doddie Weir, wearing a black and white oversized top hat, was being chaired around the pitch spraying the crowd with champagne. Significantly, on the final whistle Rob Andrew and his players headed straight for Dean Ryan and Steve Bates on the touchline and the triumvirate bounced into each other's arms at the end of a truly remarkable rise to the top for the Newcastle club. The fans indulged themselves with chants of 'Are you watching Saracens?' and 'Are you watching Stuart Barnes?' directed towards the Sky TV cameras. The new kids on the block were as brash as ever and little has changed. Sir John Hall joined his team and the fans on the pitch and Rob Andrew addressed the Newcastle supporters with a heartfelt speech in which he said: 'We have started something special. When we started this two and half years ago we were all there at ground level and the Premiership has shown that anything is possible. What we have achieved today is down to the players, management and supporters and together we have won this league in style.'

Nothing that has happened since has dimmed Andrew's feelings for that day, 17 May 1998, at The Stoop and for that season of extraordinary achievement. 'Winning the title at The Stoop was one of the highlights of my whole career playing-wise and the highlight of my career in club management' Andrew said later.

> To go through our first season in the Premiership and win the title was an unbelievable achievement and one that I believe will remain an unprecedented feat in English rugby. We were a very strong side with a lot to prove and we played some very good rugby throughout the season. A lot of our players like Gary Armstrong, Doddie Weir, Alan Tait and Pat Lam had never played in the First Division before. But they had a massive desire to prove themselves, as had the likes of Nick Popplewell, Dean Ryan and Inga Tuigamala for their new club. They were all hungry for success. Also I cannot underestimate how important it was for me personally. We had got off to a flyer with a victory at Bath in our opening game, then in the week after Christmas we had excellent back-to-back

Inga Tuigamala tells anyone who will listen that Newcastle are number one and the rest of the Falcons agree with him as the celebrations really start on the Harlequins pitch with the Premiership Trophy.

away wins at Bristol and Leicester and suddenly the idea of winning the title became more than just a dream. Steve Black, our fitness coach, said all through the season that we were the right players in the right place at the right time. More importantly, we recognised that and made the most of it. After coming through against Leicester and Bath, we knew that we had to beat Harlequins to win the title and, to be frank, I never had any doubts we would do it. It was a glorious day with the crowd in shirtsleeves and after they had a go at us early on, the result was never in question as soon as Gary Armstrong scored our first try. That took the pressure off us and we were able to really enjoy the game and play some lovely fluid rugby. I even managed to score a try myself in the second half and if anything the final 44-20 scoreline flattered Harlequins as they scored a converted try late on after we had given all our replacements a run. The incredible scenes at the presentation after the match underlined exactly what the title meant to the players, Sir John Hall and, of course, our supporters, who had travelled down in droves and were boosted by a large number of Toon Army fans who had stayed on after the FA Cup final. I only wish you could bottle those emotions and scenes and hand them on to the next generation of players to show them what it's all about. That's why you play rugby and the memories of that great day will live with me forever.

Dean Ryan manages to relieve Inga Tuigamala of the Premiership trophy as the party gets into full swing.

The Falcons bring the Premiership Trophy and the Sanyo Cup back to Newcastle and parade their spoils in the city centre.

The celebrations moved on from The Stoop to Richmond with the team bus exiting Harlequins and about to turn off for Newcastle when Dean Ryan informed the driver of his new route and there were many sore heads on arrival back in Newcastle at around 7 a.m. There were many more hangovers for the rest of the week with a string of receptions, including one by the Mayor of Newcastle, a players and wives/partners dinner and a barbecue Samoan style at the home of Va'aiga Tuigamala…and there was still one more game to play at Twickenham in the Sanyo Cup, the traditional end-of-season match between the Champions and a World XV.

On the eve of the match, Pat Lam and Doddie Weir were back in London to receive accolades as Premiership Player of the Year and Scottish Player of the Year before playing at Twickenham the next day. It was to be Pat Lam's last match for Newcastle, although no one would have believed it at the time that the Samoan captain would be transferred to Northampton before the start of the next Premiership campaign. Ironically, Lam would be playing against Springbok Marius Hurter at Twickenham and Hurter's eventual move to Newcastle would be one of the reasons for Lam's departure. It would also be Alan Tait's last game for Newcastle, with the Scotland and British Lions centre intent on pursuing his career north of the border, and he was made captain for the day in recognition of his contribution to the Falcons' cause. There was real concern amongst the Newcastle heroes about their ability to give a good account of themselves against a star-studded World XV and nothing looked less likely than that when they trailed 41-19 in the second half, having played like a side who had been celebrating for a week. Incredibly, Newcastle fought back with two tries from Lam and a winning score from Tuigamala in the 77th minute to become the first club side to win the Sanyo Cup 47-41. It was another stunning achievement and sparked another night of celebration. The teams who played that day at Twickenham were:

Newcastle: S. Legg, J. Naylor, V. Tuigamala, M. Shaw (G. Childs 62), A. Tait (captain), J. Wilkinson (R. Andrew 41), C. Simpson-Daniel (G. Armstrong 41), G. Graham, R. Nesdale (R. Horton 66), P. Van-Zandvliet (D. Barnes 41, P. Van-Zandvliet 70), R. Beattie, D. Weir, P. Lam, R. Arnold (S. O'Neill 47), P. Walton (N. Frankland 70).

World XV: P. Vaccari (Italy) rep E. Rush (New Zealand) 50, C. Williams (South Africa), S. Glas (France) rep P. Sella (France) 58, P. Sella (France, captain) rep G. Leaupepe (Samoa) 40, P. Bernat-Salles (France), D. Knox (Australia) rep A. Thomas (Wales) 66, A. Pichot (Argentina), C. Blades (Australia), R. Ibanez (France) rep R. Cockerill (England) 49, M. Hurter (South Africa) rep D. Garforth (England) 55, H. Strydom (South Africa) rep T. Coker (Australia) 40, W. Waugh (Australia) rep H. Strydom (South Africa) 58, M. Gianvielli (Italy) rep F. Pienaar (South Africa) 58, F. Pienaar (South Africa) rep. S. Latu (Japan) 40, T. Strauss (South Africa).

The referee was S. Piercy (RFU).

It was a fitting end to a glorious season for Falcons and most of the Newcastle team opted for a summer off to recharge their batteries – the Scottish contingent of Doddie Weir, Gary Armstrong, Alan Tait, George Graham and Peter Walton had all decided they would not be going on tour to Australia with Scotland during the summer, a move that

Tony Underwood and Doddie Weir display the Premiership and Sanyo Cups to an admiring crowd and manager Rob Andrew.

met with the approval of Sir John Hall who had made it clear he would not stand in the way of any of his players if they wanted to tour with their national sides. Tony Underwood's injury-ravaged season continued when he also ruled himself out of England's tour to South Africa to try and build up his suspect knee, but Jonny Wilkinson and Garath Archer did go on England's ill-fated tour to Australia, New Zealand and South Africa where England, denuded of their experienced players and fulfilling another crazy schedule, were thrashed unmercifully. It was to take Wilkinson some time to recover from the mental and physical scars of the mauling and he ended up with nasty ankle injury in New Zealand. Tim Stimpson was also on the tour but as a Leicester player, his Newcastle contract having expired and he left having signed a three-year deal with the Tigers resisting any temptation to have swipe at his former club. 'I have been out in the wilderness and at times the whole situation was quite bleak because I thought I could have added something to Newcastle's league and cup performances. There were times when I felt a bit of an outsider although I was delighted when Newcastle won the title. There are no hard feelings. What Newcastle did in eighteen months was remarkable but I felt I had to move on for the sake of my international future and it was an incredibly frustrating period.'

14
LAM MOVES ON

There was little time for Newcastle Falcons to savour their Premiership triumph and they would not reap any reward by being in Europe with England's clubs boycotting the Heineken Cup in yet another row over money, television right and representation.

Newcastle were fully behind the boycott as were all the EFDR clubs presenting a united front, but privately the Falcons hated the idea of not being in Europe as English Champions. It's a truism that nothing ever stands still, especially in sport, and Newcastle's capacity to upset the applecart and shock the rugby world is well known but even they surpassed themselves in July 1998 when they transferred Premiership Player of the Year Pat Lam to Northampton, who paid £100,000 for the Samoan captain. Lam signed for the Midlanders on a three-year contract and Saints director of rugby Ian McGeechan was delighted at his capture. 'Pat Lam is an outstanding player and we're happy to have him. Everything happened quite quickly, I don't think a lot of people knew he was available. He has a tremendous attitude and he has all the skills – he could even play in the back line. He's also a leader and we're looking to him to give us what he gave Newcastle' added McGeechan. Lam had scored 16 tries in 33 appearances for Newcastle and his controversial transfer was a major shock for the Kingston Park supporters, although Welsh club Neath had attempted to sign him the previous season.

Northampton completed the deal while the twenty-nine-year old was in Samoa preparing to lead his country against New Zealand A. Many reasons have been advanced for Lam's transfer, among them the official line, which was that manager Rob Andrew had signed Springbok prop Marius Hurter, whom he saw as an essential improvement to the Falcons' pack, and Hurter's arrival meant Newcastle would have three overseas players on their books in Lam, Hurter and Va'aiga Tuigamala. They were allowed to field only two in the league and cup and, while Tuigamala was in line to become English-qualified because of residence, that could take some time to come through. On that basis Andrew said he felt obliged to sell Lam and he also said he felt that perhaps Lam's best years were behind him. However, it was rumoured that Andrew had been backed into a corner and told to sell Lam because the Sporting Club directors saw the Lam deal as good business. Andrew has always been very much his own man and it's difficult not to see the final decision to sell Lam as being his. There certainly had been difficulties over negotiating a new deal for Lam at Newcastle and the money he felt he could command as Premiership Player of the Year, but Andrew wanted Hurter and if he felt he had to shed one of his overseas players to make way for the South African then it would not be Inga Tuigamala.

Lam said he did not want to leave Kingston Park but, once he realised Andrew was intent on selling him, he decided the time was right to move on. On his return from captaining Western Samoa on their tour to New Zealand, Lam met up with Ian McGeechan and England back row Tim Rodber, Northampton's captain, and the deal was

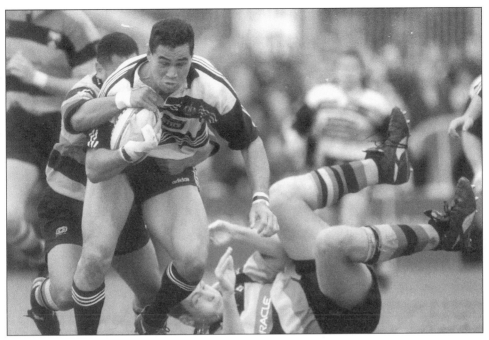

Pat Lam's departure to Northampton was a major shock. There would be no more sights like this as Lam in a Falcons shirt thunders into the opposition defence head on.

Pat Lam makes the point that he was happy to stay at Newcastle but when it became obvious that Newcastle were ready to sell him he moved on to Northampton.

done. 'I would have stayed with the Falcons for the same money if they had offered me the security of a three-year contract' said the Samoan captain, 'but they wouldn't and when Northampton made me such a good offer I felt I had to secure my family's lifestyle and future. However, money is not a priority with me and never has been. It was the lifestyle and living in Newcastle that I enjoyed and I enjoyed playing for the Falcons.'

Lam had asked Andrew at the end of the Falcons' Division Two promotion season for talks about signing a new contract but nothing was decided then or during the Premiership winning season, despite inquiries by Neath, Wasps and Northampton regarding the player's availability. It was while Lam was in Samoa that he learned from his agent that Newcastle were looking to sell him. 'I rang Rob and he told me that he could not match what Northampton were offering me and I told him I wasn't concerned about that and that I still wanted to stay, but then it became clear that he was signing South African prop Marius Hurter and that would mean three overseas players – Marius, Inga and me – when you are only allowed to play two in the league. I realised then that he was looking to sell me for that reason and I really had no choice after that. Everything then happened very quickly although I did check with the Newcastle board and they confirmed that Rob had told them he wanted to sign Hurter and then I knew I had to go. Obviously, I was upset and so was my family and the most disappointing thing was that I felt I had been very loyal – and I've always believed in loyalty – and I believed in the vision of Newcastle. I played in games at the end of the Premiership-winning season when I was injured and risked my career with Samoa to help the Falcons win the title and I was a bit disappointed with the way things turned out.'

Lam's departure was the first hint that the Falcons' Championship-winning side was about to break up and in the space of a few months Lam had been joined by Alan Tait and Richard Metcalfe in moving on while props Nick Popplewell and Paul Van-Zandvliet had to quit because of injury. Following the departure of Tim Stimpson to Leicester and John Bentley back to Halifax Blue Sox, it seemed the days of the big-name players at Kingston Park were numbered but, of course, that was not to be the case. However, things did look a little bleak when Alan Tait completed his move to new Scottish district team Edinburgh Reivers. The thirty-four year old British Lion said that 'It was no secret I was keen to return to Scotland, not least because I know that in terms of talent we're not that far off the pace. Some people seemed to think that Newcastle were almost invincible last season, but I know differently. There were a lot of what I call normal players, good solid blokes.' One of those was Richard Metcalfe, a 7ft 1in second row forward, who was frustrated at the lack of first team opportunities at the Falcons, where he had established internationals Garath Archer and Doddie Weir in front of him. 'I want to stay at Newcastle but I also want to further my rugby career and play for Scotland' he said. 'Rob was very understanding and said he would place me on the transfer list and inform other Premiership clubs'. Metcalfe eventually also signed for Northampton and went to establish himself in the Scotland side but his departure was seen as a worrying trend that Newcastle were unable to hang on to their players; although Andrew did unveil a number of new faces along with Marius Hurter, the new South African prop, including England Under 21 winger Michael Wood, who signed from West Hartlepool, Wharfdale's prop Ian Peel, who would quickly win England

Under 21 honours and Moseley's England Under 21 full back Peter Massey and refuted rumours that his playing budget had been severely trimmed. 'I'm happy with the budget' he said, 'Very, very happy. It's true we will not be running a second team but we will have a senior squad of twenty-six players, an elite Under 21 side and we will be extending our Under-19 and Under-17 sides in partnership with local clubs.'

There was also another departure – a sad one, albeit understandable – when former club captain Neil Frankland, who had been on loan to Northern, decided to sign for the North Division One club, which ended the Yorkshireman's fourteen-year spell with the Newcastle club. It was not a happy period for the Falcons. Everything they touched had turned to gold the previous two seasons and now it seemed they could not put a foot right with players leaving, scrapping their second team (which raised a few eyebrows) and then a public relations disaster when they decided to withdraw their £5,000 funding of the mini-rugby section just six weeks before the start of the youngsters' season. It was bad timing at best and a crass decision at worst and alienated many parents and members. The mini section were fortunate to be able to move into nearby Bullocksteads, the home of the reformed Gosforth club and Northumbria University, and also to find sufficient funding to continue operations, but Newcastle gained little from the exercise other than bad publicity and a blow to their reputation and their claim to promote rugby in the North-East.

15
THE GATESHEAD EXPERIENCE

As expected, the Falcons announced they would be playing their home games in the 1998/99 season at Gateshead International Stadium, and Falcons director David Campbell said 'Two new stands will be erected behind each goal line which will provide us with 6,000 covered seats and another 4,000 open seats – something which is impossible at Kingston Park at the moment – and Gateshead have carried out extensive drainage work on the pitch with which we are very happy.'

It was not, however, to be a happy stay, with Newcastle failing to reach the high standards of the previous season and occasionally being forced to switch to Saturday because of Sky TV demands. That didn't help attendances and neither did the weather, which was invariably poor. Gates which were so disappointing that the Falcons would abandon Gateshead and return to Kingston Park after only four matches.

There was another blow when prop Paul Van-Zandvliet was injured in car crash on the Tyne Bridge. Van-Zandvliet suffered whiplash and a broken foot when his car was hit by a tank transporter. The initial amusement that a player whose nickname was Tank being involved in an accident with a tank transporter quickly wore off when it became clear the injuries were such that he would not be ready for the start of the season and eventually Van-Zandvliet had to accept he would not play again and retired to become manager of a pub in Alnwick, which he named the Falcons Rest.

The one piece of good news was that Jonny Wilkinson was fit again after the abortive tour to Australia, New Zealand and South Africa. England were hammered 76-0 by Australia and 66-22 by New Zealand, during which Wilkinson had been stretchered off with an ankle injury. The Newcastle youngster had made a physical recovery but there were worries his confidence had taken a big knock going into the season where he was expected to assume a more high-profile role with the Falcons. Wilkinson was as rational and calm as he always appears to be on the field when he said 'Of course, there are things I will never forget, but only because remembering them will help make me a better player. I'm not one for looking back unless I can use the experience to improve my game. It's important I learn how to cope with extra responsibilities and how to become a controlling force as we try to change the way we are playing the game and alter our style.' It wasn't the first hint that the Falcons were seeking to move away from the forward-orientated style that had won them the title, even through they had been the Premiership's top try scorers in their league triumph with coach Steve Bates and Rob Andrew deciding the way forward was for a more fluid game based on moving the ball quickly through the backs.

Wilkinson wore the number 10 shirt and Andrew wore 12 in their opening game at the Madejski Stadium but they alternated at fly half and Andrew handed the kicking role to the nineteen-year-old Wilkinson. It was not an auspicious start for the youngster, with a 50 per cent success rate, including one miss from in front of the posts, as Richmond won

The Newcastle players get used to the surroundings of Gateshead International Stadium after the Falcons decided to play their home games there in the 1998/99 season. It was to be a short-lived experiment.

Watched by Alan Tait, Rob Andrew chips the ball behind Phil de Glanville and Jeremy Guscott as Newcastle play Bath at Gateshead Stadium in appalling weather and, as a result, a disappointing crowd.

comfortably 41-29; but in typically resilient fashion Wilkinson kicked five out of five as the Falcons won their next match 19-17 at home to Bath in front of a disappointing crowd of 3,452 (the game being moved forward 24 hours to a Saturday because of Sky demands being an undoubted factor).

Newcastle's unbeaten home Premiership record disappeared in their next match when Conor O'Shea scored a try and kicked an injury-time touchline conversion for London Irish to win 23-21, and there was another poor crowd of 4,184. Then the Falcons just survived a late comeback by West Hartlepool in their derby clash, winning 24-19, and just four weeks into the season there were questions being asked whether they were a spent force. Rob Andrew dismissed talk of a crisis but did admit there were problems. 'To be honest we were on such a high from the previous season that we had to come down some time' he said. 'We had a lot of changes, a lot of things happening and we didn't fly out of the blocks at the start of the season but any side that can beat Bath as we did is competitive.' The Newcastle manager emphatically refuted rumours of players being unhappy over money issues but did admit that 'There was an issue of bonus payments during the summer. There were two elements to the players' bonus. The first was for winning the Premiership and that money was paid out. The second was for qualifying for Europe and while the players kept their side of the bargain as it were, the fact that the English clubs boycotted Europe meant that the cash was simply not available. Some people were less than amused but it's a real world out there.' Newcastle's share of the cash from television sponsorship would have been £750,000 had the English clubs been in Europe. Instead, it went down from the £480,000 they received the previous season to under £400,000. 'But we still had a healthy playing budget' said Andrew. 'It wasn't slashed to pieces or cut right back or anything like that. There were lots or rumours flying around and the exaggeration was huge. Perhaps it was the price we had to pay for winning the title when people didn't want you to or expect you to.'

Crisis? What crisis? Thus went the official line and there was a change of tune from the critics when the Falcons beat Wasps 27-19 in superb style in their next game and looked every inch champions, but another crowd of less than 4,500 rang the alarm bells in the corridors of power at St James's Park – particularly in light of the fact that it was costing around £25,000 to stage every match at Gateshead and the break-even figure on the crowd was 7,000. It didn't take a rocket scientist to work out that Newcastle were losing money hand over fist by playing South of the Tyne. Rumours of a return to Kingston Park were sparked afresh when the bulldozers moved in to level the ground on the West side of the ground for what clearly was the setting up of a new, bigger temporary stand and club officials finally admitted late in October that Newcastle would, in fact, be moving back to Kingston Park after playing Saracens at Gateshead on 31 October. Newcastle chief executive Ken Nottage stated that 'The decision was not take lightly. Gateshead is an outstanding environment in which to play rugby but sadly due to the disappointing attendances at the games, which is mirrored throughout the country, we have to make hard business decisions.'

While the Gateshead debacle was a temporary blip, and the return to Kingston Park was greeted with relief by many fans and attendances did start to climb again, they were nowhere near what they had been the previous season and would remain down as the

Falcons struggled through the season looking for the spark that made them virtually unbeatable the previous season and battled to come to terms with trying to play their more open style. They were still without new prop Marius Hurter, whose arrival was delayed because he was contracted to finish the season with Western Province who were still involved in the Currie Cup, South Africa's national cup competition. The worst news that Newcastle could have received during this difficult period would have been the departure of Rob Andrew. That didn't happen but the next worst thing did, with Steve Black being spirited away by Wales coach Graham Henry.

Newcastle coach Steve Bates had often said that Newcastle could get along without himself or skipper Dean Ryan (and they had to face life without Ryan sooner than they might have expected) but Bates reckoned the man they could least afford to lose would be Steve Black, who was much more than a fitness adviser. Black was, and is, an innovator, instinctive psychologist and deep thinker about fitness and the mental side of sport – talents not immediately recognisable in a smiling, bearded Pavarotti look-a-like with an off-the-wall sense of humour that some people find difficult to understand. To the Falcons players he was friend and father-confessor as well as fitness coach and Steve Black is one of the very few people who could talk to tough and macho rugby players about love, respect and admiration for team-mates and get away with it – his departure was a severe blow to both the Falcons players and management.

Newcastle immediately lost their next match at Gloucester 41-32 and while they bounced back to win at Bedford 29-22 and crush Saracens 43-12, they were edged out 25-20 at

The loss of Steve Black to become Wales' fitness coach was a shattering blow for the Falcons in a season of major setbacks.

Harlequins where they had clinched the title just six months before and were wallowing in mid-table, looking uncertain at times and were clearly not finding it easy as defending league champions. The departure of players like Pat Lam and Alan Tait, injuries, a change of playing style and then Steve Black's departure all contributed, although things did look a little better when Marius Hurter arrived. The 13-cap Springbok immediately brought stability to a struggling Falcons pack with his 6ft 2in, 18st frame but it was very much a case of two steps forward and one back, with the arrival of the big South African overshadowed by the loss of skipper Dean Ryan, who would be out of the game for three months following a neck operation to remove a ruptured disc which was pressing on a nerve. There were fears Ryan would be out for the rest of the season and, in fact, he was, but it ceased to be Newcastle's problem as Ryan was never to play for them again; he moved on to Bristol to become number two to Bob Dywer in a surprise transfer that caused a few jaws to drop given the war of words between the former Leicester supremo and the Falcons No.8 the previous season.

Ryan's departure ended a partnership with Rob Andrew that had spanned many years at Wasps and which had taken the Kingston Park club through their transformation from moribund Second Division Newcastle Gosforth to Premiership champions Newcastle Falcons and his departure was another massive blow – although a parting of the ways had been on the cards for a while, with rumours that the Newcastle board were reluctant to give Ryan more than a one-year extension to his contract in the light of his neck problems while Ryan wanted a new three-year deal. Ryan's transfer was completed early in January 1999 and Ryan, who had been recalled briefly to the England side the previous season, said 'It's a wrench to leave Newcastle after so much success over the last three years, but I am still ambitious and I want to develop my rugby career and Bristol have offered me that opportunity and it's a challenge and an opportunity I don't think I can turn down.' Rob Andrew insisted he had tried hard to keep Ryan at Newcastle, the manager stating that 'He has been instrumental in the success of the Falcons over the last three years and that resulted in the championship last season.'

Ryan wasn't the only player to be facing career-threatening injury problems as Tony Underwood, after what had seemed to be a confident and competent return to both the Falcons and the England side, injured his knee again in the England match against South Africa. This would keep him sidelined until the following January. Newcastle were still capable of excellent rugby, as their 45-35 win over Northampton showed, but it was a problem of consistency as they lost 31-18 at Leicester and they seemed unable to string together a run of results. However, there was a major boost for the club when Rob Andrew announced that British Lions and Scotland second row Doddie Weir had signed a new four-year contract that would tie him to Newcastle until the age of thirty-two. Saracens had been tracking Weir for several weeks, believing him to be unsettled at Newcastle, and Andrew had not been best pleased by the attentions of the London club, making a formal protest to EFDR (English First Division Rugby) for what he considered an illegal approach. After Weir had re-signed, Andrew said 'It's the biggest thing that has happened to the club since we signed Inga Tuigamala and probably bigger because of the message it sends out to everyone in the game. I'm delighted because it is a very big statement by the board of their faith in the future of the professional game and we have

There were more injury problems for Tony Underwood when he suffered another knee injury, which would sideline him in the 1998/99 season until January.

Doddie Weir shows the sort of form that convinced Rob Andrew he couldn't let him go and the Scotland lock signed a new four-year contract with the Newcastle club in the 1998/99 season.

shown that we not only want to keep a quality player like Doddie Weir at Kingston Park but that such a quality player wants to commit himself to play for us. I fully anticipate Doddie's signature will be the first of wave of new contract signings.'

Weir himself was happy with the fact he was staying in the North-East. 'I know I have made the right decision' he said, 'things were complicated by Saracens' interest but I am happy to have re-signed. I love the Falcons and I love the North-East and I will be staying among friends.' Just when everyone was writing off the Falcons as championship contenders they won 30-15 against Sale and 29-13 against West Hartlepool; but they then lost 16-14 at London Irish and their chances of retaining the title finally disappeared when they went down in four of their next seven games and faced several weeks without the services of Doddie Weir when he fractured an ankle in the Scotland *v.* Wales Five Nations Championship match. However, the problems the Falcons were having on the field were dwarfed by the crisis that hit the Kingston Park club early in February 1999 when Sir John Hall's Sporting Club announced they were pulling out of their involvement with rugby, ice hockey and basketball.

16
THOMPSON TAKEOVER

Rumours had been flying around for months that Sir John Hall was wanting to cut his losses and his ties with the game because of mounting debts and growing disenchantment with Rugby Union and its seeming inability to move as fast as the millionaire Tyneside businessman would like. Club officials and Sir John – who was certainly not as 'hands-on' in his approach as he had been the previous season – had consistently maintained it was business as usual. All that changed during the first week in February when the Falcons were told by Douglas Hall and Freddie Shepherd that Newcastle United were wanting to cut their losses and get out of rugby at the end of the month.

Douglas Hall and Shepherd informed David Campbell, a Falcons director and also on the board of management of the Shareholders Association (who controlled 24 per cent of the Falcons shares) of their decision to write off what has been estimated as Sporting Club debts of up to £9m. and sell their shares for a nominal amount. Manager Rob Andrew called a meeting of his players to break the news to them and there were some worried faces after the meeting although Andrew insisted it would business as usual as far as the Falcons were concerned.

It looked as though the loss-making Sporting Club was being offloaded because of the high-powered negotiations that were going on involving Newcastle United and the proposed sale of Douglas Hall's shares in Newcastle United to cable TV company NTL. It left the Falcons in a precarious position as they had less than month to try and find a new backer and maintain their position as one of the major rugby clubs in the country.

The crisis deepened as it emerged there was a 1 March deadline or the club could be wound-up. Although Cameron Hall's decision was a shock and major blow to the Falcons, no-one was quick to point the finger of blame. Quite the opposite, because the legacy left by the Halls was a massive one. Andrew admitted that the news of the Halls pulling out was a shock and after a week of trying to keep the club running on an even keel, he said 'As soon as it came out it created uncertainty and speculation started. There are so many rumours. In a week, we have merged with West Hartlepool, been bought by Cardiff. I've sold six players to Saracens and I'm on the way to a new job at Richmond! It is unsettling. We've not had that rumour mill for three years because we've just been onwards and upwards.'

Andrew told his players what was happening as soon as the news broke and while several senior members of the squad said they felt better that the situation is out in the open and felt the club could now move forward, some of the younger players were naturally worried after having committed themselves to a side that might now have a limited future. 'Everybody has to look at their situation and decide what to do. I still don't know what the outcome of this will be. We may find a solution to it. I'm still very hopeful that we will, it's only days since the speculation started.' Andrew was emphatic that the Falcons did have a future and that

Had Sir John Hall (left) not gone into semi-retirement would things have been different at the Falcons? He did, however, and Rob Andrew (right) was faced with the possibility that he and his players would be out of a job by March when the Sporting Club pulled the plug on the Falcons.

circumstances had conspired against Newcastle, with Sir John's decision to retire and spend much of his time in Spain plus the political upheavals in rugby and a drop off in support for the Falcons. 'We haven't been as consistent this season, but we are making a lot of changes. We turned the corner with some of the young guys coming through after Christmas and we have played some good stuff but we have had problems about where to play and when to play. We didn't know what the season would be like and whether we would have a British League. We didn't know whether it was Gateshead or Kingston Park and two or three of our big games were moved to a Saturday because of Sky and coincided with Newcastle United playing at home. But there are still signs that if we can get a few things sorted then we can get back to those expectations where we had 9,000 to 11,000 people watching at the end last season and whatever the shakedown is in the next six to twelve months I still think the top ten or twelve sides in England will be fully professional. I think the players at the very highest level have to support international rugby. We've been fighting for European Cup revenue and from Allied Dunbar and European Cup sponsorship, each Premiership club should be looking for a minimum of a million pounds. If you then have 10,000 spectators at every home game with a minimum of fifteen home games, then you don't have to be a genius to work out how much income is coming into a club. We've only attendances to that level occasionally at Newcastle but some clubs are getting near that 10,000 mark. You need to be getting attendances up to that and you need to get your sponsorship and television income sorted.'

The 1 March deadline to find a new backer raised the possibility of the club finding itself in a similar position to that experienced by Bedford earlier that season when players and staff were not paid. It prompted a frenzy of activity and whether the deadline was simply a ploy by Cameron Hall to make things move quickly is largely immaterial now but at the time it did increase tension. There was also much political in-fighting behind the scenes as different factions jockeyed for position and tried to come up with a realistic plan to save the club from what could have been bankruptcy and closure. The Shareholders Association, who owned 24 per cent of the shares to the Halls' 76 per cent, were to take an increasingly influential position because of the rights they had obtained when they sold the club in 1995. One was a veto preventing the Falcons moving from Kingston Park without their permission, which effectively prevented a sale to a club like Cardiff who, at the time, were desperate to break away from the Welsh Rugby Union and become part of the Allied Dunbar Premiership, and were actively looking at trying to buy an English club for their league rights. Another right the Shareholders' Association had was the option to purchase the Hall's shares and take back the club for themselves and this led to the resignation of David Campbell as one of the shareholders' two nominated directors on the Falcons board, citing a conflict of interests because he was believed to be representing an outside group trying to buy the Falcons.

Shortly afterwards he was the first to lodge a formal bid to buy the 76 per cent shareholding from Cameron Hall on behalf of a consortium of Tyneside businessmen. That brought into play the clause that gave the Shareholders Association a thirty-day option in which to match Campbell's bid and buy back the majority shareholding themselves. In the event, the shareholders association did not have to take that step themselves because of the arrival of David Thompson on the scene. Campbell had talks with David Thompson and brought him into the arena of discussion, but Thompson moved camps and allied with the Shareholders' Association, who were working with another North-East millionaire, Paul Mackings, and Rob Andrew. Thompson's decision probably had much to do with the fact Campbell's plans for Newcastle did not necessarily envisage Andrew staying as head of playing operations. The Shareholders' Association reacted swiftly to Campbell's bid with Col Morgan, chairman of the board of management of the shareholders, confirming that Rob Andrew and the Association were working on a package which would 'ensure the long-term future of the long-term survival of the Newcastle Falcons as one of the top rugby clubs in the country.'

Paul Mackings had been interested in getting involved with Newcastle some time before but had been rebuffed by the Halls, and he became part of the consortium backing West Hartlepool and was their representative on EFDR after a short spell as West's chief executive. Both Campbell and the Shareholders' Association were also actively talking to Northumberland County – who still had close to £3m in the bank following the sale of their county ground some years before – and they were looking at setting up a centre of excellence and, inevitably, the question of a merger with either Northern or West Hartlepool was also raised.

Northern, who had been offered £5m for their McCracken Park ground by a builder, did not rule out re-locating at Kingston Park in a ground-sharing move, but they were understandably reticent about committing to anything with the situation so volatile at

David Thompson rides to the rescue of the Falcons. Thompson (with rugby ball) with his 'team', who put together the takeover package at Kingston Park in an amazingly short space of time. From left to right: Paul Mackings (chief executive), Chris Appleby (Upton Nichol Williamson), Rob Andrew, John Gray (Falcons director), Simon Watts (Dickinson Dees), Peter Clark (Dickinson Dees) and a former first team player, Phil McClintock (Upton Nichol Williamson).

Kingston Park. West Hartlepool, some thirty miles down the A19 were certainly interested in the possibilities of the two clubs getting together to form a North-East super club but West chairman Andy Hindle said that any possible merger would have to be 50-50 and the new club would have to play on a neutral site to placate both sets of supporters. One of the proposed sites was Sunderland AFC's new Stadium of Light. Hindle confirmed West's former chief executive Paul Mackings had been in talks with David Campbell but a merger between to the two clubs was never a real prospect; quite apart from the geographical difficulties of deciding where such a club would play and what it would be called, West were in even deeper financial trouble than the Falcons. By the following May they had been relegated from the Premiership, been forced to make most of their players redundant and player-manager Mike Brewer was on his way to Italian side L'Aquila. Forced to make a Company Voluntary Agreement whereby they would pay off a portion of their debts to creditors, West slid straight through Division Two and into Division Three to effectively end the prospect of Premiership rugby returning to the Hartlepool and Teesside area.

It was somewhat ironic that Newcastle and Richmond, the two clubs at the forefront of the rugby revolution and big spenders in the early days – and whom many considered had bought their way into the First Division – were both in trouble and facing extinction. Richmond's owner Ashley Levett had also gone the route of the Halls and withdrawn his backing after losses of £8m. The London club went into administration and was eventually swallowed by London Irish. Many people at the time were betting that it would be Newcastle and not Richmond who would disappear, especially when the 1 March deadline came and went, although disaster was averted as David Thompson was in the process of taking over the club. On Thursday 11 March 1999 he was officially unveiled as the Falcons' new backer.

The new owner made one thing very clear right from the start and that was the key role Rob Andrew would continue to play at the club. Thompson, a former prop forward with another Newcastle club, Novos, and a multi-millionaire who made his money from a wide range of companies including management consultancy Druid Systems, also announced he had made Andrew a full director of the new company running the Falcons as well as player-manager. 'I believe Rob Andrew is essential to this rugby club' he said. 'I hope when he ends his playing career he takes over more and more onerous tasks and ultimately that he will end up in my position. I'm a Geordie and we only do things if it is commercially viable. There's no point in going into this if we can't make the Falcons commercially viable and I'm convinced, with Rob's help, we can.' A self-confessed rugby nut, who was still involved in junior coaching, Thompson joked he had 'only bought the club so I could get my hands on some of the Falcons kit' but stressed he believed in the long-term viability of rugby in England and the North-East. He added that Andrew's playing budget had already been approved. Besides Andrew and Thompson himself, Paul Mackings was also appointed a director and chief executive and John Gray, representing the Shareholders' Association, was named the fourth director of the club. Thompson's take-over cost a nominal £1, as that was what is cost to buy the Cameron Hall shareholding, and Newcastle United also wrote off the Sporting Club debts, which were said to be in the region of £6 million in the case of the Falcons. The Halls also left after signing a £100,000 sponsorship deal and there's no doubt that the takeover by Thompson could not have taken place had they not allowed the club to start with a clean sheet. Assets included Kingston Park and a playing squad conservatively valued at around £3m-£4m. Thompson was said to have made a seven-figure commitment over five years. In fact it was much more.

Falcons skipper Gary Armstrong was quick to applaud Thompson's takeover and pledged his continued support for the club. 'Dave Thompson is a passionate rugby man – as passionate about the game as Rob Andrew and the rest of the lads are' he declared. 'There has obviously been uncertainty at the club since the turn of the year and I am one of the players who will be out of contract at the end of the season. I have been knocking on Rob's door but he hasn't been able to do anything as his hands were tied. Now he has his budget for next season and is a full director, contracts can be negotiated and I, for one, want to sort things out as quickly as possible. I love it here, I'm certain the club has a great future and I want to be part of it.' Andrew wasted no time in getting down to negotiations and issued a hands-off warning to the rest of the Premiership predators, who had been

He's staying. Rob Andrew issued a hands-off warning to the rest of the Premiership, underlining he would not be letting players like Inga Tuigamala leave after David Thompson took over the club from Sir John Hall.

waiting to cherry-pick the Falcons best players if the club had gone to the wall. 'We aim to keep our major assets and that includes Inga Tuigamala and Jonny Wilkinson' said Andrew. 'We will be negotiating with all the players who come out of contract this year as soon as possible to ensure that we can keep a very talented squad together. We have to keep our top players here as our ambition is to be among the top sides in British and European rugby and that may mean we have to buy more top players. I don't see Jonny Wilkinson being out of contract in May as a problem. It's a fact of life and you have to address it. You don't have to be a genius to realise I want to keep him here.' Tuigamala, like Armstrong, immediately pledged his future to Newcastle, insisting he saw himself as seeing out his career with the North-East club.

Thompson's style was entirely different from that of Sir John Hall and he had a major advantage in that he was a rugby man and understood both the game, the diversity of characters which inhabit it and the difficulties it can have in reaching conclusions and decisions because of its traditional structure. Significantly, Thompson became a member of the EFDR (English First Division Rugby) executive and was also drafted on to the Club England Task Group, chaired by Rob Andrew, which was given the brief of producing a format for the game in England for the twenty-first century.

17
SIGNED AND SEALED

Newcastle's new owner was as good as his word and by April Rob Andrew had signed both Jonny Wilkinson and Gary Armstrong to new contracts. Scottish skipper Armstrong signed a new three-year deal, while Wilkinson, the hottest property in British rugby, felt able to commit himself to at least another twelve months at Kingston Park. He was later to extend that contract after the World Cup in Wales.

Wilkinson, still only nineteen at the time, had been the hero of England's win over France the previous week with seven penalties in a 21-10 to equal Rob Andrew's record. He signed his new one-year contract with Newcastle on the eve of the match against London Scottish and promptly celebrated by scoring another 23 points as Newcastle won 43-20. Wilkinson was believed to have quadrupled his earnings to £80,000-a-year and said 'I'm pleased to have all the speculation sorted out. I'm happy to stay with Newcastle. I asked for a one-year deal and that's what they have given me. There have been other clubs making inquiries but I always wanted to stay here. I wouldn't say it was an easy decision because there has been so much speculation but it is the right rugby decision for me. Rob did not have to do a great deal of persuading, but I did talk to my father and one or two others about what I needed to do. It's best for me to stay here and it's a good agreement. I'm just trying to make sure I secure my future in the game, that I don't end up finished at twenty-five or twenty-six and that I keep on developing. This is the best place for that. There is a great mixture of experience and youth here and I have the utmost confidence in Rob and Steve (Bates).'

Wilkinson had joined Newcastle as a seventeen-year-old and had been tracked by Saracens (amongst others). Newcastle knew they had to pay to keep him but Andrew believed it was money well spent 'I am absolutely delighted both Jonny Wilkinson and Gary Armstrong have agreed to stay with the club. They are both massively influential here and have done so much to establish the Falcons as one of the leading clubs in the country. This is the first stage of the continued development of the club following the change of ownership under Dave Thompson and I am currently talking to all the other players who are coming out of contract. Ideally, I would have liked Jonny to have signed for longer, but I can understand his position. We now have to prove to Jonny this is the place to be for the longer term. There were one or two other clubs interested in signing him and that's always the case when players of Jonny's quality are coming out of contract, but deep down I don't think Jonny ever wanted to leave.'

Gary Armstrong, rated as equally important to the Falcons, was delighted that his future has been secured. 'Everyone who knows me understands how much I love this club and I fully expect to see out my playing career here.' It seemed that the Falcons had turned the corner with a new owner at the helm and, while they were out of the Premiership title race, they were still very much in the running for a place in the European Cup after the English clubs announced they were ending their boycott of the championship – too late for Newcastle to play that season as Premiership champions,

One of the first signatures Rob Andrew made sure he had after Dave Thompson's takeover of the Falcons was that of Gary Armstrong, who signed a new three-year contract.

but in time for the clubs in the top half of the table to realise there was something for them all to fight for. Furthermore, the Falcons still had the opportunity to land their second successive major trophy when they beat Richmond 20-3 to reach the final of the Tetley's Bitter Cup, where they would face Andrew's former club and the previous season's beaten finalists Wasps.

Would their luck hold as it had on their way to the Premiership title when they were incredibly injury-free, apart from Tony Underwood's problems, as they chased European qualification and Tetley's Bitter Cup? It would not. They ran into a casualty list which was to have a catastrophic effect on their European Cup hopes. Most of the damage was done in Falcons' controversial 34-33 defeat at Wasps when the London club scored their winning try in the second minute of injury time after referee Robin Goodliffe decided, on the advice of his touch judge, that Inga Tuigamala had tackled Gareth Rees late. It was a marginal decision at best and Newcastle coach Steve Bates was furious with the match officials as Wasps kicked into the corner, rumbled over for a try from the line-out and Alex King's conversion made it 34-33. What was even worse was that Rob Andrew was injured trying to prevent the try. He was led off as King kicked the conversion and it turned out he had dislocated his left shoulder, which had to be put back in under anaesthetic. 'That's me out for the season' said the Newcastle manager. 'The shoulder hurts a bit but the result hurts an awful lot more.' It meant Andrew would miss out on the Tetley's Bitter Cup final against his old club Wasps, but the more immediate worry was a must-win home Premiership game against Richmond after another very physical game against Wasps which left Newcastle with five key players in trouble in the middle of another period of

Rob Andrew on the sidelines in a pensive mood after dislocating a shoulder against Wasps, which was to cost him a last appearance in the Tetley's Bitter Cup final at Twickenham against his former club.

three games in eight days and the prospect of having to play Harlequins on the Tuesday before the Cup Final and Saracens the Thursday after the following month. This was clearly a ludicrous schedule and it's hardly surprising Newcastle ended up with no trophy and no European Cup place at the end of it. Sadly, this is not the first time one of England's top sides have had to play an exhausting end-of-season programme with a great deal at stake.

It did look as if Newcastle had enough left in the tank when Richmond were dismissed 47-14 with Gary Armstrong scoring a hat-trick, but Richmond were a pale shadow of the side they had been with a bleak future facing the club and the players after failing to find a new backer. Then Gloucester were turned over 39-15 to take the Falcons into seventh spot in the Premiership and in with real chance of breaking into the European scene, but Tim Stimpson returned the Kingston Park to kick Leicester to the title and Newcastle just about out of European contention. Stimpson kicked seven perfect penalties in the Tigers' 21-12 win and it was sweet revenge for a player shown the door by Newcastle. To take the Falcons' title from them on their own patch was particularly sweet for the England full-back and particularly galling for Newcastle. 'When Newcastle won the title at Harlequins I was in the party' said Stimpson, 'but I didn't drink the champagne. I passed it around to other lads. This time I might be on the bottle for four or five days!' The defeat left Newcastle with two more Premiership matches in which they might yet make it into a European Cup spot, but they would have win at home to Harlequins the Tuesday before their Tetley's Bitter Cup final date with Wasps and then at Saracens the Thursday after the cup weekend. 'We knew all along it might come down to those two games' said coach Steve Bates, 'and we will not be changing our attacking style because the way to win those games is to play the way we did against Leicester where we played all the rugby but made crucial errors.' Bates was quick to congratulate the Tigers and Stimpson and added: 'I don't think Tim was treated the way he believes he was, and the way Leicester plays suits his game. He kicked very well and he should be congratulated for that.'

Newcastle did the business against Harlequins, winning 33-23 to move back to seventh in the table but it was only thanks to late Jimmy Cartmell try and 18 points from the boot of Jonny Wilkinson that saw the Falcons through in the last 10 minutes – and it still needed one of the tackles of the season from Tony Underwood on Jason Williams in the closing minutes to prevent a certain try and the possibility of Quins stealing the game. The problem for Newcastle now was not in getting their players up for the Cup Final – the occasion itself would do that – but making sure they got enough rest before what inevitably be another massively physical game and also whether Rob Andrew would be fit for the Twickenham date. After ruling himself out immediately after suffering a dislocated shoulder at Loftus Road, Andrew made terrific progress and in just one month was considering a comeback in the final. But he ended the debate whether he should or shouldn't play on the Thursday before the final when he announced that Jonny Wilkinson would be wearing the Falcons number 10 shirt and that he would be watching from the dugout. 'I'm not fit enough to play' said a disappointed Andrew, 'and I won't be fit to play against Saracens either. I'm ruling myself out although it was very tempting to put myself on the bench for the final and think about coming on, but there are enough people around me – including my wife – telling me not to be so stupid. I want to play next season and the doctors have said I run the risk of putting it out again and that would mean an operation. It will be a strange experience being on the sidelines on Saturday. It's been hard enough recently doing that and I don't think I will know what to do with myself on Saturday. Steve Bates and a few other people keep telling me I have to get used to it and I get the feeling they are trying to tell me something!'

The final was a big day in the Newcastle club's history. The last time they had been in a Twickenham final was in 1981 when, as Gosforth, they lost to Leicester in the John Player Cup, the forerunner of the Tetley's Bitter Cup. For Newcastle's powerful Samoan and former All Blacks wing Va'aiga Tuigamala it would be a special opportunity to become the first man to pick up a winner's medal at Wembley in the Silk Cup Challenge Cup with Wigan and at Twickenham in the Tetley's Bitter Cup with the Falcons. Tuigamala had predicted that Newcastle would win the Premiership at the start of the previous season and at the start of the current season he predicted the Falcons would win the Cup – and he'd done much to make sure they would be at Twickenham with two tries against Saracens in the quarter-finals and another two against Richmond in the semi-finals. 'I've played in the Challenge Cup final and won it and it would be nice to be the first player to win finals at Wembley and Twickenham, but it's not really about me, it's about what we've been trying to do here at Newcastle with developing the club.'

Newcastle resisted the temptation to move Tuigamala from the wing to centre in place of the injured Rob Andrew and showed their faith in the youth policy by handing the number 12 shirt to England Under 21 cap Tom May after just two Premiership

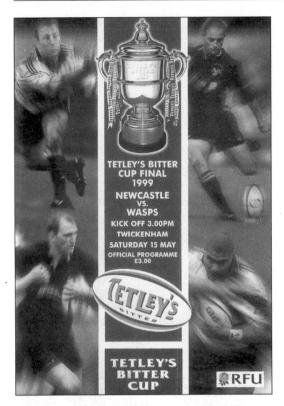

The programme for 1999's Tetleys Bitter Cup final, the Falcons' first final at Twickenham in eighteen yrears. Gary Armstrong and Inga Tuigamala are featured on the programme along with Alex King and Lawrence Dallaglio of Wasps.

Tony Underwood on the charge at Twickenham as he breaks clear against Wasps in the Tetley's Bitter Cup final.

games. It meant Newcastle would line up with a midfield of nineteen-year-old Jonny Wilkinson, twenty-year-old Tom May and twenty-three-year old Martin Shaw.

The final was a huge disappointment for the Falcons. Not so much because of the 29-19 defeat by Wasps but because they underachieved in front of a big audience – the sight of Newcastle and Scotland prop George Graham on his knees and inconsolable at the final whistle will remain an abiding memory. So will the genuine act of kindness by Graham's Scotland team-mate Kenny Logan. The Wasps wing left the celebrations in front of the stand to run over to Graham, pick him up and lead him away with an arm around the shoulders. Before kick-off, manager Rob Andrew had climbed the steps of the West Stand trying to find his seat. He looked lost and perhaps it was instead of being out there on the Twickenham pitch he had graced so often that was the problem. His team seemed to be in the same boat on the pitch where they were clearly second best to a determined Wasps side. Referee Steve Lander awarded 34 penalties, fairly evenly split at 18 against Wasps and 16 against Newcastle, but the Falcons players felt he could have awarded double that against streetwise Wasps who slowed down Newcastle's possession. 'It was intensely frustrating' said Newcastle captain Gary Armstrong. 'Wasps defended very well and they always seemed to have more defenders than we had attackers. They'd done their homework and no matter

Tom May can't believe it and George Graham is distraught on his knees as the final whistle goes at Twickenham and Newcastle lose the Tetley's Bitter Cup final and the chance of a second successive major trophy.

where we went, whether we went wide or up the middle, they always seemed to have men over. They always seemed to be on the front foot and we always seemed to be on the back foot when we were trying things. I'm not looking for excuses, but we try and play a fast expansive game and they were able to slow the ball down and that's nobody's fault but our own – they were simply better than us on the day.'

Manager Rob Andrew stopped short of directly criticising Lander, but both he and coach Steve Bates had not been happy all season with the standard of refereeing and Newcastle had seemed to suffer more than any other side from some shoddy decisions in Premiership. However, blaming Lander for the Falcons' Twickenham failure was simplistic although the game was no great advert for rugby. 'I think what we have to try to do is stop the cult in this country of slowing the ball up at the breakdown' said Andrew. 'Players are doing that and getting away with it and we need quick ball to produce an open game. That's a general comment and no criticism of Wasps. What I would like to see is someone sin-binned in the first five or six minutes of the match. Someone kills the ball for the third time in a row early in the game and he's off for ten minutes – that would make players think twice and would make them get away from the ball. At the moment, they just get constantly warned and then sent to the bin in the 78th minute when it doesn't matter.' Newcastle were chasing the game throughout as Wasps enjoyed all the breaks to lead 16-6 at half time and 19-6 shortly after the interval. When Inga Tuigamala was caught just short of the line after a 60-metre run, it was clearly not going to be Newcastle's day.

The Falcons were on the back foot from the kick-off although Jonny Wilkinson kicked a 4th minute penalty, Wasps levelling with a Gareth Rees penalty for offside twelve minutes later. Wasps moved into the lead when Garath Archer infringed at a ruck and Rees kicked the goal, and were very much running the show. In the 26th minute Alex King slid through the Newcastle midfield and outside Tom May to chip over full-back Stuart Legg and beat both May and Armstrong to the touchdown; Rees' conversion made it 13-3. On the half hour, Archer was offside and Rees made it 16-3 although Wilkinson pulled three points back just on half time. Lander then made the first of some crucial decisions which went against Newcastle. Stuart Legg fielded a high kick and Lander decided it was a Wasps put-in at the scrum when Newcastle obviously believed it should have been their ball and, from the scrum, King dropped a goal to stretch Wasps' lead. The game was running away from Newcastle and they needed a score. But despite stringing together a superb attack through Wilkinson, Tuigamala, Graham and Armstrong which had try written all over it before Wasps, cynically, went offside, Newcastle had to settle for a just penalty from Wilkinson.

Newcastle had a try in their grasp when Tuigamala intercepted in the 58th minute and raced away from his own half. It seemed he must score as he ran in from 60 metres but he was hampered by a shoulder injury and Josh Lewsey caught him right on the line to prevent him from going over. It should have been a penalty to Newcastle with a Wasps player handling the ball on the ground but referee Lander decided it was a scrum and also gave the put-in to Wasps. It was the game's big turning point and despite a penalty from Wilkinson on the hour, Rees edged Wasps ahead again with a penalty; Newcastle were really chasing the game now and had to resort

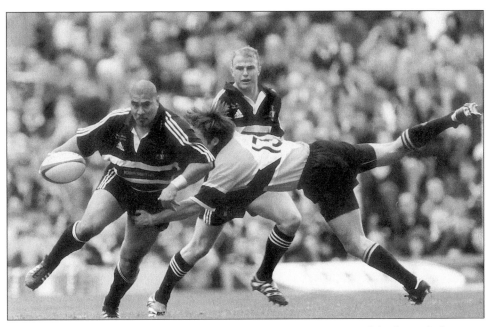

Inga Tuigamala tries to round Fraser Waters with Martin Shaw in support as Newcastle battle to get back on terms with Wasps in the Tetley's Bitter Cup final at Twickenham.

There's no way through for Jonny Wilkinson, although he has plenty of support from Garath Archer, Marius Hurter, Ross Nesdale and Peter Walton.

to running the ball from everywhere and paid for their high-risk strategy in the 77th minute when Lewsey intercepted Tuigamala's pass to Legg and shot in for the try, which Rees converted. Right on time, Tuigamala intercepted Mike Friday's pass for a try but it was too late. The teams who played in the final were:

Newcastle Falcons: Stuart Legg, Jim Naylor (Tony Underwood 41), Martin Shaw, Tom May, Va'aiga Tuigamala, Jonny Wilkinson, Gary Armstrong (captain), George Graham, Ross Nesdale, Marius Hurter (Ian Peel 69), Garath Archer, Doddie Weir, Peter Walton (Jimmy Cartmell 41), Richard Arnold, Ross Beattie.

Wasps: Gareth Rees, Paul Sampson, (Kenny Logan 46), Mark Denney (Rob Henderson 66), Fraser Waters, Josh Lewsey, Alex King, Andy Gomersall (Mike Friday 48), Darren Molloy, Trevor Leota, Will Green, Mark Weedon (captain), Simon Shaw, Lawrence Dallaglio, Joe Worsley, Peter Scrivener.

The referee was Steve Lander (RFU).

Paths to the final: (fifth round) Newcastle 25 Bath 22, Wasps 53 Sedgley Park 3; (sixth round) Newcastle 32 West Hartlepool 21, Wasps 27 Waterloo 10; (quarter-finals) Newcastle 15 Saracens 0, Wasps 19 London Irish 3; (semi-finals) Richmond 3 Newcastle 20, Wasps 35 Gloucester 21.

The day wasn't over for the Falcons who were still trying to swallow their disappointment in the post-match bash in the Twickenham Rose Room when the worst possible news began to filter through from the Bath *v*. London Scottish game. Newcastle were expecting Bath to win but not by a massive score as that would make their task at Watford against Saracens more difficult, but once Sunderland-born second row Mick Watson was sent off after just 40 seconds for head-butting Martin Haag, Bath went to town against a fourteen-man London Scottish and won 76-13. It meant the Falcons had to beat Saracens by a 30-point margin to pip Bath on points difference for the final European Cup spot in the Premiership table.

If it had been difficult to prepare the players in a short space of time for the cup final after playing the Tuesday before – and they'd won that game – trying to get them mentally and physically right for the coming Thursday's match at Watford was a monumental task and new owner David Thompson defused the pressure by reassuring the players that their future did not hinge on winning by the significant 30-point margin and qualifying for Europe. Thompson also made it clear there would be no cuts in the club's playing strength should they fail to qualify for Europe and thus lose out on £300,000 European Cup sponsorship money, plus the chance to cash in on gates and their own sponsorship from at least three European Cup pool games the following season. This was a laudable statement and there was a palpable degree of relief among the players who knew they had an uphill task, especially when Inga Tuigamala was ruled out of the game with injury and skipper Gary Armstrong also had to drop out of the game when his brother was taken seriously ill.

Disappointment is etched on the faces of Jonny Wilkinson and Ian Peel after they collect their losers' medals in the Tetley's Bitter Cup final.

The match ended in defeat, 40-26 and a season which had promised so much ended dismally for the Falcons. They simply never looked like achieving their target of a win by 30 points against Saracens and had the Falcons not shown real grit in the second half, the London side could have run up a massive score. 'We looked like a side who were playing their third game in ten days' said coach Steve Bates, 'and we did struggle. Basically the guys were shattered.' Jonny Wilkinson, who had been named Premiership Young Player of the Year during the week, scored 21 of Newcastle's 26 points with a try, four penalties and two conversions; he also made the other Falcons try for Martin Shaw.

18
ANDREW RETIRES

Failing to qualify for the European Cup and losing the Tetley's Bitter Cup final was a major disappointment for the Falcons, although they would again be in the European Shield (which was the European Conference by another name as the second-tier competition). Never one to look back, manager Rob Andrew was already planning for the new campaign and he'd lined up a replacement for England second row Garath Archer, who had been the subject of a bid by Bristol. Archer admitted to being torn between staying with Newcastle, who had offered him a new contract, and Bristol, where he could renew his partnership with former Falcons skipper Dean Ryan, a player he admired enormously. When it became clear his choice would be Bristol, Rob Andrew moved quickly to sign twenty-five-year-old Glasgow and Scotland lock Stuart Grimes as a replacement and also re-signed Kiwi flanker Richard Arnold on a four-year deal (including a testimonial to mark his ten years with the Kingston Park club). 'We see Stuart as an ideal replacement for Garath and he will complement Doddie Weir in the second row and Richard has always been an integral part of the Newcastle Falcons and we were not surprised when Cardiff tried to sign him' said Andrew. 'However, he's been with Newcastle since 1991 and we didn't want to see him go and we have agreed terms for another four years.'

The disappointment of not qualifying for the European Cup was not particularly assuaged by the news just before the start of 1999/2000 season that they would be in the European Shield, although the Falcons management professed themselves pleased to be involved. If they put on a brave face with regard to Europe and being in the Shield, they were aghast at confirmation that they would have to play Premiership games during the World Cup. The prospect of playing without as many as nine or ten of his top players was one that filled Rob Andrew with dismay. 'If we have to lose that many players we could have problems' he said; these words were to prove prophetic. Nevertheless, the Falcons looked in reasonably good shape with the arrival of Stuart Grimes and young players such as Jamie Noon, Ross Beattie, Michael Stephenson, David Walder, Peter Massey, Micky Ward, Ian Peel, Jimmy Rule, Hugh Vyvyan and Hall Charlton starting to come through – although there was a sad note when both their Premiership-winning props Nick Popplewell and Paul Van-Zandvliet finally conceded that injury had ended their playing careers at the age of thirty-five and thirty-three respectively.

Popplewell had played just seven games the previous season because of a foot problem while Van-Zandvliet had not played at all because of the car crash which left him with back and neck problems. 'Life goes on and you have to make choices' said Popplewell. 'Had I been five or six years younger I might not have been so philosophical but I have had a fantastic career and while it's a pity to have to pack it in, I have been able to play in both the amateur and professional era and was part of Newcastle's Premiership-winning side

Garath Archer's departure to Bristol at the end of the 1998/99 season led to the signing of Scotland lock Stuart Grimes.

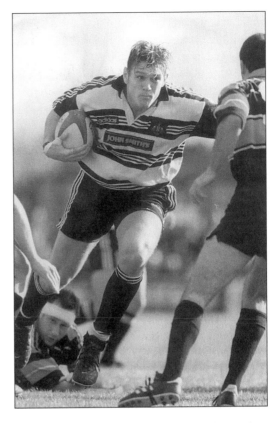

As well as signing Stuart Grimes, Rob Andrew re-signed Kiwi Richard Arnold in a new four-year deal that also included a testimonial season.

which was terrific' he added. Popplewell had been capped 48 times for Ireland and played for the 1993 British Lions. Van-Zandvliet may not have scaled the same heights but he was an integral part of the Newcastle side in their championship season and formed a formidable front row with Popplewell and hooker Ross Nesdale.

When Rob Andrew signed a new contract which committed him to Newcastle until September 2002 there was every reason to believe that the new season would bring further success for the Falcons – if they could survive the opening months without their big names who would be on World Cup duty. Andrew, England's most-capped fly half with 71 appearances, had turned thirty-six in February but seemed to have made a good recovery from the dislocated shoulder that ended the previous season prematurely for him. The prospect of semi-retirement was on the cards for Andrew when Jonny Wilkinson returned from World Cup duty with England, especially with England Under 21 fly half David Walder also being groomed as an essential part of the Falcons squad. As it turned out, Andrew was to be sidelined sooner than he thought but signing a new contract with the Falcons filled him with fresh enthusiasm. 'I'm delighted to have signed a new deal with Newcastle. I feel like we're starting all over again. Last year was a difficult one for the club. A lot of big names left the club, starting with Pat Lam in the summer and then we lost Steve Black to Wales and Dean Ryan went to Bristol and we had both Nick Popplewell and Paul Van-Zandvliet missing and they have now retired, while Garath Archer has moved on to Bristol, although we have signed Stuart Grimes, a more than adequate replacement' he said. 'When the Halls left there were huge changes within the club. That six-week period was a pretty desperate time for the club and we were lucky that Dave Thompson came along and I'm very excited about the next three or four years. We have a second opportunity, a second bite at the cherry to make professional rugby work in the North-East. We don't want to be in the same situation in three years time as we were in March because I don't think we'd survive it. But I am happy to be here for at least the next three years and I'm looking forward to finishing the job I started four years ago.'

Andrew could also point to a lot of work which had gone on behind the scenes at Kingston Park since David Thompson's takeover. A new temporary stand would be in place for the start of the season along with improvements to floodlighting, clubhouse and other spectator facilities. 'There have been a lot of changes with a great deal going on behind the scenes. We haven't really started yet – just scratched the surface – and I think we've got a very bright future indeed.' A very important part of that future was the success of the Falcons Academy, which was developing a production line of young players and four of them - Micky Ward, Hugh Vyvyan, Jimmy Rule and Jimmy Cartmell – also signed full-time contracts at the same time as Andrew signed his new deal. 'The work Paul MacKinnon, our Rugby Development Manager, has been doing over the last three years is coming to fruition – and that's the way forward' said Andrew. 'We have proved in signing Stuart Grimes to replace Garath Archer we are prepared to sign big-name players when necessary but otherwise we want to produce our own.'

Both Andrew and Tony Underwood came through the Falcons pre-season match at Manchester which was won, just, 24-20 but all the real attention was focussed on the World Cup and, from the Falcons point of view, on the number of players they would lose to the Samoan, Scotland, Ireland and England squads. Va'aiga Tuigamala would be with

Samoa, Ross Nesdale with Ireland, George Graham, Stuart Grimes, Doddie Weir, Peter Walton and Gary Armstrong with Scotland and Jonny Wilkinson with England at the tender age of twenty.

Wilkinson's meteoric rise from promising schoolboy international to World Cup star in just two years was the stuff of dreams and Falcons coach Steve Bates pointed out: 'It's amazing when you think that we brought him here to Newcastle at the beginning of 1997 and after just one full season in the Premiership, it's quite an incredible achievement to be in the England World Cup squad.' It was Bates who had been instrumental in bringing Wilkinson to Newcastle after he had met the youngster at Lord Wandsworth School in Hampshire. 'The headmaster brought him to my attention and suggested he might be the mainstay of out first XV and I thought "yeah, yeah" and was expecting to meet someone brash and arrogant, someone who was full of himself and thought he was the star of the show' said Bates. 'Jonny could hardly have been more different. He was very humble and very quiet, very slight in those days but obviously very talented.' Bates knew he had found a special player and when he moved to the North-East he told Andrew they needed to keep in touch with Wilkinson because he was going to be a very good indeed. 'When he left school he came to see us and his original intention was to take a year off just to see how he would go but before the end of the season he was in the first team. He's a workaholic and we have to drag him off the training pitch sometimes.'

The World Cup was to prove a disappointment for England and for Wilkinson, who was left out of the line-up for the quarter-final against South Africa until it was too late. By the time the Falcons number 10 came off the bench to inject some much-needed invention into the England side, Jannie de Beer's record 5 drop goals had sunk England's World Cup dream without trace in a 44-21 result. It says much for Wilkinson that he able to bounce back from the disappointment of the World Cup and doubts over his ability to run the show for England, to be the central figure in England winning the first Six Nations Championship the following April, breaking all sort of records along the way.

Surely all doubts about his ability for international duty have been banished forever with a mercurial performance against the Springboks on England's summer tour to South Africa in the summer of 2000. Wilkinson's 8 penalty goals in a 27-22 victory in Bloemfontein (which levelled the series at 1-1) set a new individual England Test record and he also kicked a second-half drop goal for good measure. Had Wilkinson made it nine penalties out of nine, it would have equalled the world Test record held by Welshman Neil Jenkins, Kiwi Andrew Mehrtens and Japan's Keiji Hirose. Typically, he said afterwards that he didn't realise the missed kick would have equalled a world record.

The World Cup was nothing but trouble for the Falcons. They were missing seven players because of the tournament in their opening Premiership game at Gloucester, although Scotland did release Doddie Weir to play in the match as they felt he needed to get a game under his belt before the World Cup started. Newcastle lost 31-16 and it was start of a very difficult season which saw the Falcons flirt with the possibility of relegation as they drew two and won just one of their first ten Premiership games. It wasn't until the end of the December when they beat fellow strugglers Sale 12-6 and then won at Harlequins 15-12 the following January that the Falcons looked capable of avoiding the relegation play-offs. It was a tough period and tough baptism for the Falcons younger players who had to step into the gaps left by World Cup calls. It might have been different but for the fact they had to do it without Rob Andrew at the helm as a player.

Andrew's career finally came to a close not at the end of a glorious international win or lifting a cup at Twickenham, but on a Monday morning in Newcastle on a training pitch. It was 20 September when another dislocated shoulder in a training accident led to an immediate visit to the specialist and, on his advice, Andrew retired from playing. It was the same shoulder that had cost Andrew his place in the previous May's Tetley's Bitter Cup final. Although it was put back in, the thirty-six year old was told he was facing an operation if he wanted to continue one of the most illustrious playing careers in the history of English rugby. Andrew's retirement was exactly four years to the day that he had been unveiled by Sir John Hall as the man to take Newcastle into the brave new world of professional rugby. In that time as player-manager he had led the Falcons to promotion from Division Two, the Premiership title and the Tetley's Bitter Cup final. His absence on the field would leave a huge gap and one the inexperienced Falcons side would find hard to fill while shorn of their World Cup players.

'When I was told the only real alternative was to have an operation, I thought long and hard about it and decided it was time to go' said Andrew. 'Everyone has to retire sometime and, to be honest, I was going to call it a day at the end of the season anyway. I'm a bit disappointed and frustrated over the way it has happened, but these things do happen. I just hit a tackle bag and fell to ground, landed on my elbow and the shoulder came out. I think someone up there is trying to tell me something. I wasn't meant to play in the Cup Final in May and now this has happened. I was just hoping I could get through the next six weeks and help the club out until Jonny Wilkinson was back from England's World Cup campaign. I will just have watch from the sidelines now. It won't be easy – I'm not a good spectator!'

It was a sad end to a marvellous playing career, during which Andrew enjoyed a golden decade at the top in the international game. 'I've had a wonderful time' said Andrew, 'and there have been many highlights. I would single out England's 1991 Grand Slam – the first by England for eleven years – as the main one from a team point of view and the winning drop goal against Australia in the 1995 World Cup as the personal high.' Born in Richmond in North Yorkshire, Andrew attended Barnard Castle School along with Rory Underwood and made his senior club rugby debut with Middlesbrough, while still at school, before going on to Cambridge University where he won his Blue at both rugby and cricket (as a left -handed batsman and right arm bowler). His playing career spanned club sides Nottingham, Toulouse, Gordon in Sydney and Wasps and he scored a drop goal 50 seconds into his England debut against Romania. He went on to become England's most capped fly half (71) and record points scorer (396) and played for the 1989 and 1993 British Lions as the records fell to his golden boot. He kicked a world record-equalling 30 points against Canada, became, at the time, England's highest-ever points scorer (beating Jon Webb's record of 24 points in the Grand Slam decider against Scotland at Twickenham) and kicked *that* drop goal against Australia in the World Cup quarter-finals at Cape Town.

Falcons coach Steve Bates knew Newcastle would not only miss Rob Andrew as a player, but they would also miss his other equally important qualities. 'We will miss him

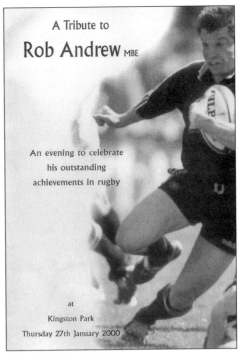

A Tribute to

Rob Andrew MBE

An evening to celebrate
his outstanding
achievements in rugby

at

Kingston Park

Thursday 27th January 2000

Rob Andrew's enforced retirement from rugby after a second dislocated shoulder was a real blow to the Falcons.

A special dinner to celebrate Rob Andrew's remarkable career was held at Kingston Park. Among the guests were Dewi Morris, Rory Underwood and the Falcons squad and supporters.

hugely in terms of what he brings to the game as a player and also to the team. His commitment, his passion for the game has been massive.' Bates, who played alongside Andrew for Wasps and England, followed the Falcons pied-piper north from London when Sir John Hall decided Andrew was the man to transform Newcastle Gosforth. Andrew did what Kevin Keegan couldn't. He gave Sir John a Premiership-winning side in just three years. No wonder new owner Dave Thompson made sure that Andrew signed a two-year extension to his contract and, by 2002, he will have spent seven years at the helm of Newcastle. While he will be remembered for transforming the Kingston Park club on and off the field, it should be also remembered he scored 570 league points for the Falcons in 69 appearances. 'His biggest attribute was his appetite for the game, for training and what he put into it' said Bates. 'We will miss him massively in terms of his influence on the pitch. His competitiveness and complete commitment was an inspiration to those around him. He has this huge will to win. That appetite for the game was reflected in pre-season training this summer where he has trained as hard as anyone at the club, and he has constantly set the example for us all at Newcastle. Rob made a huge contribution to the game of rugby union. I played alongside Rob an awful lot at Wasps, and I think he was pretty hard done-by in the sense that people only seemed to look at his kicking qualities.' Bates' biggest worry once he realised Andrew would be standing next to him on the touchline was how he would behave! 'I'm pretty laid-back and try to remain calm but there is a difference between Rob Andrew the player and Rob Andrew standing on the touchline. He finds it very difficult – he's a little bit more emotional than me. He is not a great spectator, and can get very intense and frustrated watching a game, but his contribution to Newcastle will remain as big as it always has been.'

As if Andrew's injury and retirement wasn't enough for the Falcons to cope with, they were rocked by another major set-back when it emerged that No.8 Ross Beattie, the natural successor to Dean Ryan, would have to have a shoulder operation. The twenty-one-year-old had missed out on the Scotland World Cup squad and the shoulder had been troubling him the previous season. Not making the Scotland squad was a major blow but not as big a blow as the news he got from the specialist. 'I really did think he was going to tell me it would only be a couple of months and when he said I would be out six months, I didn't know how to react. I nearly burst out laughing because I thought it was a joke and then I realised he meant it and I was a bit upset to say the least.' Beattie would not play again until the following March following the operation but, despite missing nearly a full season, he did achieve his ambition of making his Scotland debut. It was against the All Blacks in Dunedin on Scotland's summer tour to New Zealand, the young Falcon completing a rapid rise to Test status after strong displays against the New Zealand Vikings and NZ Maoris.

The absence of Andrew and Beattie through injury plus those on World Cup duty was reflected in 56-8 and 55-6 hammerings by London Irish and Saracens and while there were a couple of draws (19-19 with Wasps and 12-12 with Leicester) with the World Cup players back in the fold after the early exits of England, Scotland and Ireland, there was yet more problems for the Falcons when skipper and scrum-half Gary Armstrong broke a collarbone in the game at Wasps. With reserve scrum-halves Allen Chilten and Hall Charlton also on the injured list, Andrew moved quickly to sign Bath's Kiwi-born scrum-half Harley Crane on loan and he also brought over South African centre Paul Baird from the Villagers club in Cape Town on trial while pursuing a major signing in Scotland's Kiwi-born centre John Leslie, who had been to Kingston Park for talks. Andrew made it clear he had money to spend to bolster his squad. He was going to need it as another of his big names was about to call it day because of injury problems.

19
UNDERWOOD CALLS IT A DAY

Tony Underwood's decision to retire was not unexpected but it was still a setback for the Falcons, coming as it did just weeks after Rob Andrew had been forced to hang up his boots. Underwood's retirement at the age of thirty, after two injury-ravaged years, brought to an end the career of one of England's finest wingers after 27 caps, the last one against South Africa the previous season. 'It's no secret that both knees have been giving me trouble but it's the left knee that has been giving me all the problems since I hurt it against Bath in 1997' said Underwood. 'At thirty, it might have been an idea to have another operation and it might have meant a few more years playing had it been successful, but it was made clear to me that I had reached the stage where perhaps if I did it again I might suffer irreversible damage.

'I have many great memories with Newcastle, Leicester, England and the British Lions and obviously winning the league title with Newcastle is one of them. I hope to stay involved with the club but I shall be pursuing my ambitions to be a commercial pilot. The North East has always played a huge part in our family life. Both my dad and my brother Rory were born in Middlesbrough, Mam lives in Barnard Castle where I was educated and my wife Heidi comes from Darlington. That's why it was lovely to sign for the Falcons. We felt we were coming home.' Tony, like his brother Rory, a pilot with the RAF, had always been interested in flying and had been taking lessons for some time before the end of his playing career came along. He was one of the very first big name players to move to Newcastle and Rob Andrew paid tribute to his former England colleague for that.

'Tony, along with Gary Armstrong and Doddie Weir, was one of my first big signings when I came to Newcastle and he gave the club credibility and I will always be grateful to him for that. He was also instrumental in creating the culture of success at the Falcons and his signing persuaded other players that we were serious about the future of the club.' First capped for England against Canada in 1992, Tony was a member of the England Grand Slam side of 1995 and played in the World Cup that year in South Africa and he also went on the 1997 British Lions tour to South Africa – where he scored 7 tries in eight games and played in the third Test against the Springboks in Johannesburg. He will be forever linked with All Black winger Jonah Lomu (as is any England player who was on the field for that fateful World Cup semi-final in Cape Town in 1995 when Lomu exploded and scored four tries in a 45-29 hammering of England) and Underwood admits: 'There was an element of naivety in our approach to Jonah. He'd made an impact when New Zealand played Japan but the general opinion was that maybe anyone as big as him would do it against such opposition. I was asked before the game if I was confident and I said yes – any player would. But I'd had a good season, I'd toured with the Lions and felt on top of my game. However, we played a loose game and turned over a lot of ball. The amount of space we gave Lomu was manna from heaven for him. We repeatedly gave him twenty yards of space to run in with us on the back foot. But I wasn't the only England player he literally ran through. There were plenty all over the park.'

Both Gary Armstrong and Doddie Weir had their injury problems as the Falcons went through a nightmare crisis with players sidelined in the 1999/2000 season. Armstrong fought back after a broken collarbone while Weir suffered a partial dislocation of his right shoulder as Newcastle's season threatened to end in chaos.

Underwood's retirement was another setback and the problems were piling up thick and fast for the Falcons as they slumped to second bottom of the Premiership following a 45-12 hammering at Bath, despite the return of the majority of their World Cup players, although Wilkinson was recovering from a leg injury. It was a performance Andrew described as 'unacceptable' but stressed there was no need to panic, with the Falcons about the embark on their pool matches in the European Shield against Narbonne, Dunvant and Aurillac. Ironically, Newcastle's European performances were to be far better than their Premiership displays and Wilkinson turned in a five-star performance as the Falcons won 20-19 in Narbonne and the return the following January 19-11. Dunvant were hammered 45-26 and 51-10 and Aurillac were crushed 55-7 but got their revenge 17-10 in the New Year which sent the Falcons into a quarter-final away tie at Pau which they would find a game too far.

While their European form was laudable, the Falcons could not reproduce it in the Premiership and there was a 16-15 defeat at home to Harlequins and a 37-5 loss at Northampton. The injury nightmare continued with Scotland lock Doddie Weir suffering a slight dislocation of right shoulder and Gary Armstrong's comeback in the much-needed 12-6 win over Sale lasting just 15 minutes before he damaged his shoulder again. Fortunately, it was not a recurrence of his broken collarbone and he was back three weeks later in the 15-12 win at Harlequins and with an OBE in the New Year's Honours list. A 41-8 Tetley's Bitter Cup win over Moseley also cost the Falcons their number one hooker Ross Nesdale for the rest of the season because of neck injury that required an operation. 'I got hit from behind with a tackle and received a bit of whiplash' said Nesdale, 'but then I had a stinging, tingling sensation in my arm and my fingers went numb and it still felt odd after I'd come off.' A

George Graham's season also ended early, but the bustling prop was still judged the Falcons' player of the season by the 24 percenters and the Keith Pattinson Journal Trophy judges.

In the wars. Ross Nesdale's unflinching commitment saw his season end early when he had to go into hospital for a neck operation on a damaged disc.

specialist confirmed Newcastle's worst fears. Nesdale would need an operation and would not play again that season. It left Newcastle wondering what else could go wrong. The answer was plenty, as the Falcons lost Scotland prop George Graham also with a dislocated shoulder during the Six Nations Championship, prompting Andrew to move into the transfer market and sign both Mike Howe, a New Zealander on London Irish's books, as a replacement for Nesdale and Harlequins prop Alan Yates as cover for Graham. The injuries threw a great deal of responsibility on the Falcons young players and they responded magnificently. By the end of the season the likes of Micky Ward, Ian Peel, Tom May, Jamie Noon, Michael Stephenson, Hugh Vyvyan and Jimmy Rule had become vital members of the senior squad and a genuine threat to the established players.

Manager Rob Andrew, who had been recruited by the RFU through Fran Cotton's Club England set-up to put together a Task Group (it would include Falcons owner David Thompson) with the brief of the producing a plan for English rugby, was still able to find time to wheel and deal in the transfer market and his ability to persuade big name players to commit themselves to Newcastle – with the help of Dave Thompson's money – was again underlined when he completed the signing of Kiwi-born Scotland centre John Leslie after weeks of negotiation. Leslie was playing for Japanese club Sanix Fujiyama on a three-year contract and the former Otago player was able to secure his release simply by giving them notice. With South African Paul Baird's trial period coming to end without his having convinced Andrew that he should sign him, Leslie arrived at Kingston Park a year to the day after the plug had been pulled by the Sporting Club. Leslie signed a three and half year deal and said: 'I came to Newcastle because of the potential the club has and the chance to play alongside talented players like England fly half Jonny Wilkinson. When I decided I wanted to be based in Britain, I weighed up all the options and Newcastle was by far the most attractive because they are a club who have the potential to go places and they are a really friendly club.'

It was an enormously significant signing and quite rightly was hailed as a landmark by Rob Andrew. It certainly helped him persuade Jonny Wilkinson to sign a two-year extension to his contract early in February which would keep him at Kingston Park until 2002. 'We made Jonny an offer just before the World Cup' said Andrew. 'He didn't speak to any other clubs but he wanted to get the World Cup out of the way and like many other England players it's taken him about nine months of their time and energy, and Jonny has been trying to get his head together since the World Cup and he's now sure that Newcastle is where he wants to be for the next two and half years. He obviously feels there is a future here and when we get him and John Leslie together we can really go places.' Leslie's signing certainly was a clear signal that Newcastle were planing for the future, even if things were not going well on the field.

There was one downside to the Leslie signing. Although he was Scotland captain and obviously qualified to play for Scotland, Leslie does not hold a British or European Union passport as he was born in New Zealand and that meant he was classed as an overseas player, which gave Newcastle a problem as they now had three 'foreign' players on their books – Leslie, Inga Tuigamala (Samoa) and Marius Hurter (South Africa) – and only two are allowed

Scotland's captain, New Zealand-born John Leslie, was a major signing for manager Rob Andrew in the World Cup season, although an ankle injury prevented him from playing a full part in the 1999/2000 season.

England fly-half Jonny Wilkinson, with mentor Steve Bates, was happy to sign a two-year extension to his contract in January 2000 after learning that Rob Andrew had signed John Leslie.

The granting of Inga Tuigamala's British qualification after living in the UK for six years solved the problem of foreign players for Rob Andrew and meant that he would now be able to play Tuigamala, South African Marius Hurter and Kiwi John Leslie in the Premiership together.

to play in Premiership matches. Tuigamala had applied for a British passport as he had lived in the UK for six years but his application would not be granted by the Home Office until mid-April The problem of having to perm two from three with regard to Tuigamala, Leslie and Hurter would only trouble the Falcons briefly as Leslie aggravated the ankle injury he'd received playing for Scotland in the World Cup and would need another operation. Newcastle wisely decided to protect their asset by standing him down, sorting out his ankle problem and aiming to have him fit for the start of the 2000/2001 season.

Close defeats at home to Bath 20-16, Wasps 36-30 and Leicester 34-26 kept Newcastle struggling in the Premiership and ended any hopes of a mid-season charge up the table and into the European Cup and there seemed to be no end to the catalogue of injuries as Scotland back row Peter Walton followed Ross Nesdale into hospital for a neck operation that would also bring his season, and eventually his playing career, to a premature end. Joining the walking wounded on the sidelines late in February was prop George Graham who dislocated a shoulder scoring a try for Scotland against Italy, prompting Andrew to despair of ever being able to put out a full strength side that season. 'This injury jinx just won't go away' he said as Newcastle got back to winning ways with a 23-20 victory over Bedford – with Wilkinson scoring all Newcastle's points, overshadowing John Leslie's debut.

There was also a new star on the horizon with Jamie Noon being called up for England training alongside Wilkinson ahead of the Six Nations Championship match in Italy. The Falcons and England Under 21 centre was named in the England squad for the Hong Kong Sevens and was clearly being fast-tracked by Clive Woodward and ear-marked as one for the future. Noon was one of several players coming out of Paul MacKinnon's Falcons Academy and the spin-offs also saw Northumbria University, with several young Falcons in the side, go on to win the Halifax BUSA Championship against Loughborough at Twickenham while Newcastle's Under 21 side defeated the touring Nike New Zealand U21 team – which prompted an invitation from coach Sid Going, the former All Blacks scrum half, to the Newcastle Under 21s to tour New Zealand during the summer.

In a rare display of anger, Andrew lashed his side after their poorest showing of the season in a 34-8 defeat at home to Wasps and he told the players they should 'go and apologise to David Thompson and thank him if he still pays their wages this week'. The words of Andrew, who was named as Newcastle Sports Personality of the Year a few days later, had a dramatic effect as the Falcons defeated Saracens 15-6 in a classic game of rugby with Wilkinson again scoring all the points with three penalties and a drop goal with both his left and right boot. It was cheeky in the extreme but the sort of arrogant skill only great players have and display without thinking. However, all the good work against Saracens was thrown away with a shock defeat 32-22 at Bedford, who hadn't won a game all season, and it raised the very real prospect of the Falcons being dragged into the relegation play-off zone along with Sale and Bedford. It meant a major re-think on Newcastle's European Shield quarter-final tie in Pau. With the European Cup organisers making it clear that the Shield winners would not qualify for the Heineken Cup the following season, the tournament had been robbed of much of its attraction. That and the fact the Falcons were facing three games in a week for the fourth time that season, prompted Andrew to rest his big names for the French game with one eye on the Premiership match against London Irish the Tuesday after the quarter-final in Pau. It was mathematically possible for Bedford to overtake Newcastle if they won all their remaining league games and the Falcons lost all theirs. It was unlikely, but Andrew wasn't about to take any chances and, not surprisingly, Pau won the quarter-final 36-20. Andrew's decision was justified when London Irish were beaten 28-23 to ease the tension and Andrew underlined just how important that was. 'Make no mistake, relegation would have been a disaster for this club' he said. 'Having seen all that's been happening and watching all the structures going into place for next season, for us to blow it and miss the party would have been too much to bear.'

Andrew had dragged Newcastle through possibly the most difficult eighteen months in the club's history. It would have been easy for him to have walked away when Sir John Hall's Sporting Club pulled out but, encouraged by the arrival of David Thompson as the club's new owner, standing down was a non-starter for Andrew. 'I've always said the professional game would take five years to sort itself out and as far as I'm concerned it starts next year and we had to be part of it and that meant staying in the first division. I make no excuses for the team selection at Pau in the European Shield. Had we won at Bedford the previous week it would have been different – that's why I was so upset at the Bedford result – but we could not take any risks in France with the London Irish game being so vital. The players reacted well and performed in Pau and also against London Irish and that's all credit to them, the backroom staff and everyone connected with the club. To have that spirit after a very difficult eighteen months with a change of owner, the World Cup problems and injuries says a lot for this club. What has happened over the last eighteen months is not a sob story, it's a fact. But we've hung in there and we're seeing a club being born. And as far as the long-term goes we are now feeding ourselves with players and that's creating a huge spirit within the club.'

Andrew is the first to concede that the star-studded side he put together with Sir John's money which won promotion and then the Premiership title was unique because it was at the birth of rugby professionalism and he was literally able to pick and choose the players he knew and wanted. 'You just couldn't do that now. You have to grow your own' he added.

20
BLACKIE'S BACK

There was a familiar figure back on the touchline in Pau with the return of Steve Black from Wales. Black had only a watching brief at Pau but was to resume his post as the club's fitness adviser and there was a real buzz around Kingston Park with his return from Wales after turning down three Premiership soccer clubs and one Southern Hemisphere rugby country ready to pay big money for his services.

'It's great to be back' said Black, who spent eighteen months with Wales but decided enough was enough after being subjected to vitriolic criticism by a some of the Welsh media and some ex-players over allegations he was moonlighting by helping Fulham with their fitness training. It mattered not that Black was helping an old friend, Paul Bracewell, and doing it in his own time, he was judged guilty without trial by some sections of the media and the concerted campaign which followed by a couple of newspapers to find anything they could use against him eventually persuaded Black he didn't need the aggravation and he resigned.

'Graham Henry did not want me to go and did all he could to keep me with Wales and said I was the best fitness coach he'd ever worked with – we forged a real partnership in those eighteen months,' said Black. 'We won 11 games in a row, became the first Welsh side to beat South Africa and the first Northern Hemisphere side to win a series 2-0 in Argentina, which isn't bad is it? It was only a small group of people who turned things sour and it's fair to say I was upset about what some of the media said and did, but I was more concerned about what they were saying about some of the Wales players and the way they were trying to find out things in my background and about my family.' Not all the newspapers in Wales wanted to see Black go and a campaign run by one attracted 4,500 letters of support, but Black had made up his mind and it was back to Tyneside to the club that he helped take to the Premiership title two years ago. 'It is great to be back and the potential at the Falcons is enormous. We were the top club in 1997/98 and my task is to not only help us get back to that position of pre-eminence again but to make sure we create a rugby dynasty here.'

Black's return was also to have an immediate bonus as Andrew ended the season as he had started it – by a signing a big name player, snatching England wing Liam Botham from under the noses of Harlequins who were convinced they had the Cardiff wing in the bag until a phone call from Black.

Andrew had tied up the signing of a new three-year contract by Springbok prop Marius Hurter to ensure the stability of his front row and there was feeling that the end of the season couldn't come quickly enough as the injury problems which had stalked the Falcons all season continued to bedevil them right up to the end of the 1999/2000 campaign, as did their patchy form with a 30-11 defeat at Bristol, a terrific 36-28 win against Gloucester (in which Jamie Noon, Tom May and Michael Stephenson came of Premiership age and Wilkinson collected another 26 points) and two defeats at Sale 45-17 and against Northampton 32-23.

Steve Black's return from Wales was a massive boost to Newcastle and he was soon back in harness with the Falcons players, including Inga Tuigamala.

Falcons new boy Liam Botham with his England team-mate Jonny Wilkinson, looking forward to his first season with Newcastle.

John Leslie suffered another setback to his hopes of making an impact at the end of the season with Newcastle when he needed another minor operation to remove some floating cartilage from his ankle.

John Leslie underwent keyhole surgery on his ankle to have a piece of floating cartilage removed and that ruled him out of Scotland's tour to his homeland New Zealand. Scotland second row Stuart Grimes would also miss the trip and didn't play in the Falcons final three Premiership games because of a back problem. Andrew had also allowed England A wing Jim Naylor to go on loan to Halifax Blue Sox to see if he could make himself a new career in Rugby League, although Naylor eventually signed for newly-promoted Rotherham. The Newcastle manager was obviously restructuring his squad for the following season as he stepped in to sign Liam Botham, persuading the England youngster to turn down Harlequins at the eleventh hour after that phone call from Steve Black.

Botham jumped at the chance of signing for Newcastle after Andrew offered a three-year deal and the opportunity to return to the North East. Botham had been with Cardiff for three years, in which time he had won a Welsh Championship medal and been courted by Wales supremo Graham Henry – prompting England coach Clive Woodward to step in and make it plain that Botham had a future with the country of his birth. That sparked Botham to seek a move back to the Premiership and he looked all set to join Quins, but Steve Black had worked with Botham while with the Wales set-up. 'My first objective was to get back into the Allied Dunbar Premiership after two and a half years with Cardiff to further my England chances' said Botham. 'I had been speaking to a couple of clubs and was close to signing for Harlequins when, out of the blue, I got a call from Blackie, whom I knew well from his time as Welsh fitness coach, asking if I was interested in joining Newcastle. To say I was interested is a real understatement as both my wife Sarah Jane and I are from the North East and not only are Newcastle a tremendous club but it was also a chance to come home. Rob Andrew then rang me and apart from a few contractual ins and outs that was it – I was a Newcastle player. It is a dream move for me. It's great to be back in what I consider my homeland and joining a club that has so much exciting and exceptional talent. I'm looking forward to working with players of the quality of Inga Tuigamala, Jonny Wilkinson and John Leslie and exciting young players like Jamie Noon. That's going to be really important. Everyone at Newcastle has been disappointed with recent performances, but there is every reason to expect that we can get back up where we were when the Falcons won the title.'

The Falcons would be Botham's second Premiership club in the North East as he started out with West Hartlepool before moving to South Wales. 'Cardiff gave me my chance as I was hardly a semi-professional, never mind a professional at West' added Botham. 'They gave me the opportunity to be a professional rugby player and I have gratefully taken it by the scruff of the neck. I know I have still got a lot to learn but hopefully my career will go from strength to strength.' Although Botham undoubtedly inherits his sporting ability from his father, Ian, he gets his love of rugby from his mother's side. 'I was introduced to the game by my grandfather and first started playing at his old club, Thornensians near Doncaster. I continued playing rugby as well as cricket at Rossall School in Lancashire and I have been lucky to have had the opportunity to choose between the two sports when it came to pursuing a professional career. I have no doubt my choice was the right one, although I know I still have a long way to go and I will be keeping my feet firmly on the ground. I am also looking forward to training with Blackie and learning from the experience of coach Steve Bates and Rob himself.'

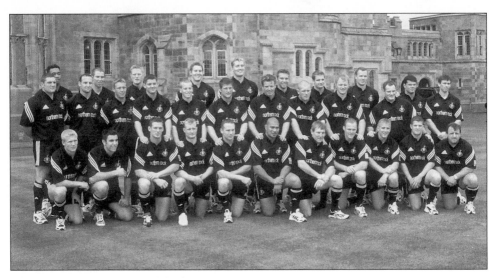

The Newcastle Falcons squad ready for the 2000/2001 season.

A week after signing for the Kingston Park club, Botham learned he was included in Clive Woodward's England party to tour South Africa during the summer. 'We tried to sign Liam when he was leaving West Hartlepool but he'd already signed for Cardiff' said Andrew after unveiling Botham at Kingston Park on 18 May 2000. 'It's a good signing for three reasons – he has undoubted playing ability, as he has proved in three seasons with Cardiff and England A, he's a very, very ambitious young Englishman – and that's what we're about at Newcastle – and, thirdly, he wants to be in the North East because he feels this is his home and I'm very pleased about that. There's no doubt that he's a man on a mission to play for England and the people we've spoken to have not said a bad word about him. Steve Black thinks very highly of Liam and says he has Jonny Wilkinson's application and anyone who has Jonny's application will do for me. I am very impressed with Liam and he has handled the pressure of being a Botham from a very young age. He adds another young quality English back to the club and it again shows that we can go into the market and attract the right man when we want him. We did it with John Leslie in the middle of the season and again with Stuart Grimes last summer. Our policy is quite clear in while we are all about producing our own players to create a Kingston Park dynasty, it takes time and we are not afraid of going out and getting an experienced star when we need him.'

21
WALTON'S WOE

The changes in the Newcastle squad as the season drew to close gathered pace with England A centre Martin Shaw moving to Sale, who had just been taken over by new backer Brian Kennedy, and flanker Steve O'Neill deciding it was the right time to return to his former club Blaydon. While Shaw and O'Neill made the their choice voluntarily, there was no such option for Scotland back row Peter Walton, who was given the news he dreaded in June after another visit to the specialist following his neck operation.

The thirty-one-year-old Scottish international, capped 24 times for his country, was told he should retire. 'Everything was going well following my neck operation until I began feeling pins and needles again in my arm and hand' said Walton. 'I saw the specialist and he confirmed that although the op had been a complete success there were other problems lower down in my neck which meant another operation and he said I shouldn't play again as the risk was too great. I was upset to say the least. I felt I had another two or three years left as a player but it's not to be and I think it will hit me hardest when all the boys are back to start pre-season training and I can't join them.' Walton was not lost to the Falcons with manager Rob Andrew offering him a job as forwards coach with the Newcastle Academy and also having an input with the senior squad. 'I had six good years with Scotland and played some good stuff with Northampton and Newcastle, with whom I won the Premiership – and there aren't many players who can say that' added Walton. 'Rob has talked with me about helping to coach the young forwards in the Academy and this is something I want to do as I think I have a lot to offer as a coach.'

Andrew paid tribute to Walton when he said: 'Peter has been a huge influence on the Falcons and there is no doubt his retirement leaves a massive hole in our back row. He played a big part in our Premiership title-winning season in 1997/98 and was always capable of making the very hard yards close to the scrums, rucks and mauls. It is a massive blow to Peter but he was advised that playing on was simply not worth the risk. We won't be losing him though as we have a very talented group of young forwards, especially in the back row, and I believe Peter is the ideal man to bring them on.' Walton's retirement prompted Andrew to sign Worcester's back row forward Jim Jenner, London Irish flanker Andrew Mower and Wigton's Irish Under-21 cap John Gardiner on trial for the start of the 2000/2001 season and, as ever, Andrew's preparations for the new campaign saw several changes in the Falcons squad. He signed Tongan international wing Epi Taione, who had been playing for Tynedale in North Division One, and offered full-time contracts to England Under 21 caps Jamie Noon, Tom May, Michael Stephenson and David Walder plus Hall Charlton, Allen Chilten and Gareth Maclure as well as hooker Mike Howe and Scotland Under 21 wing/full back Ross Cook who had been with Northampton.

As an overseas player Taione gave Newcastle the problem again of having three such players on their books with Marius Hurter and John Leslie both holding overseas passports, but

Peter Walton's career with the Falcons and Scotland was ended when a neck operation appeared to have cleared up a back problem but further complications led to his retirement and he joined the club's coaching staff.

Is it a bird? Is it a plane? No, it's Flash the Falcon, the Newcastle mascot who made his re-appearance during the 1999/2000 season and looks set to be flying high with the team in the future.

Andrew said: 'Epi is an investment for the future and we will see how he develops as a full-time professional.' Andrew announced a slightly bigger squad of thirty-one and that the Falcons would be fielding a second team for selected matches. The new arrivals inevitably meant departures and full-back Stuart Legg signed for French club Biarritz and England Under 21 winger Michael Wood and England Under 21 hooker Ritchie Horton were released.

The departure of full back Stuart Legg severed another link with the Falcons' Premiership-winning side of 1997/98. Legg, a near ever-present that season, was a victim of the rapid rise of nineteen-year-old Michael Stephenson, while the season's leading try-scorer Martin Shaw had effectively been replaced by two other young meteors, Jamie Noon and Tom May, and the writing was on the wall for Michael Wood as soon as Liam Botham was signed. 'It was hard on Stuart Legg and Michael Wood, in particular, as he worked very hard on his game but once we signed Liam we had to adjust' said Andrew. 'The speed with which our younger players are now coming through means all our full-time professionals will have to look over their shoulders and won't be able to rest on their laurels.'

As he announced his new squad, Andrew felt said he believed the 2000/2001 season would see the Falcons turn the corner and begin to realise their potential and challenge for top honours again. 'You simply can't legislate for the injuries we had last season and with George Graham, Ross Nesdale, Stuart Grimes and Martin Leslie all back fully fit, it is a case of having four new signings who hardly played last season. I am very excited about our prospects next

Big things will be expected from the England Under-21 quartet of Tom May, Micky Ward, Jamie Noon and Michael Stephenson in the next few years.

Just a few of the galaxy of international stars that Newcastle manager Rob Andrew has assembled at Kingston Park. From left to right: Doddie Weir, Marius Hurter, Jonny Wilkinson, Liam Botham, John Leslie, Ross Beattie.

season and if everyone is fit and playing well we will be able to compete with anyone in the Premiership.'

Who would bet against that, with players of the quality of Jonny Wilkinson, John Leslie, Va'aiga Tuigamala, Gary Armstrong and Liam Botham – plus Jamie Noon, Michael Stephenson and Tom May vying for a place in the back line and a revitalised Falcons pack with all their experienced internationals fully fit and on song? If the season does end with the Falcons tasting success once more, it will be another stop on a remarkable journey, a roller-coaster five-year ride from second division obscurity to Premiership champions, Sanyo Cup winners and Tetley Bitter Cup finalists and who knows what else in the future – European Champions perhaps?

APPENDIX
HONOURS, OFFICIALS AND CLUB RECORDS

Honours

Allied Dunbar Premiership
Division 1: Champions: 1998.

Allied Dunbar Premiership
Division 2: Runners-up: 1997.

Courage League Division 2
Champions: 1993.

Tetley's Bitter Cup (formerly John Player Cup, Pilkington Cup) Winners: 1976, 1977.
Runners-up: 1981, 1999.

European Shield
Semi-finalists: 1998
Quarter-finalists: 2000

RFU Northern Merit Table
Winners: 1977, 1981.

Sunday Telegraph Pennant
Winners: 1971, 1973, 1974, 1977.

Northumberland Senior Cup
Winners: 1928, 1956, 1960, 1962, 1963, 1964, 1966, 1967, 1968, 1969, 1971, 1972, 1973, 1974, 1975, 1976, 1977, 1978, 1979, 1980, 1981, 1982, 1983, 1985, 1986, 1987, 1990, 1991, 1993 (trophy shared with Tynedale after 6-6 draw after extra time), 1994.
Runners-up: 1932, 1936, 1950, 1951, 1957, 1961, 1970, 1984, 1988.

Northumberland Senior Shield
Winners: 1954, 1955, 1962, 1964, 1966, 1968, 1974, 1978, 1979, 1980, 1983, 1992, 1993, 1994.

Northumberland Junior Cup
Winners: 1921, 1929, 1930, 1931, 1947, 1950, 1959, 1964 (shared with Percy Park), 1965, 1968, 1978, 1979, 1980, 1989, 1992, 1995.

Northumberland Junior Shield
Winners: 1895, 1913, 1921, 1922, 1939, 1947, 1957, 1959, 1960, 1961, 1966, 1967, 1968, 1970, 1978, 1982, 1983, 1984, 1989, 1993.

Northumberland Junior Trophy
Winners: 1991, 1992, 1993, 1995.

Northumberland County Sevens
Winners: 1957, 1959, 1960, 1963, 1972, 1974, 1982, 1991.

Middlesex Sevens
Runners-up: 1977.

Journal Trophy
Winners: 1976, 1977, 1978, 1979, 1980, 1981, 1982, 1984, 1986, 1987, 1995.

Northern Merit Table
Winners: 1977, 1981.
Runners-up: 1978, 1982.

British Lions

1924 J H Bordass
1955 A R Smith
1966 R J McLoughlin
1971 P J Dixon
1974 R M Uttley
1983 S Bainbridge

1997 A Tait
1997 G W Weir
1997 T Underwood
1997 T Stimpson
1997 J Bentley

Internationals

England

1897 G C Robinson
1920 A M Smallwood
1971 P J Dixon
1972 R M Uttley
1977 M Young
1982 S Bainbridge
1983 C White
1996 T Underwood
1996 T Stimpson
1996 G Archer
1997 R Andrew
1997 J Bentley
1998 D Ryan
1998 J P Wilkinson

Scotland

1955 A R Smith
1974 D F Madsen
1978 R W Breakey
1982 J A Pollock
1996 G W Weir
1996 G Armstrong
1996 P Walton
1997 G Graham
1997 A Tait
2000 S Grimes
2000 J Leslie
2000 R Beattie

Ireland

1962 R J McLoughlin
1996 N Popplewell
1996 R Nesdale

Samoa

1996 V Tuigamala
1996 P Lam

Tonga

1998 E Taione

Barbarians

1898 G C Robinson
1933 G S Waller
1954 A R Smith
1956 M A Pearey
1962 R J McLoughlin
1962 G Blackett
1969 P J Dixon
1972 R M Uttley
1972 D F Madsen
1973 D Robinson
1975 B Patrick
1977 M Young
1977 C White
1979 S Bainbridge
1979 J Butler
1982 P Simpson
1982 J A Pollock
1995 P Walton
1996 N Popplewell
1996 G W Weir
1996 T Underwood
1996 T Stimpson
1996 R Andrew
1998 D Barnes
1998 M Shaw
2000 J Naylor

Officials 1877-2000

Gosforth Football Club

Season President Club Captain Secretary
1877-78 Rev Allan Charlton W S Williams S F Bates
1878-79 Rev Allan Charlton W F Fenwick S F Bates
1879-80 Rev Allan Charlton W F Fenwick S F Bates
1880-81 Rev Allan Charlton W Farr S F Bates
1881-82 S H Farrar W Farr R Smith
1882-83 S H Farrar W Farr W Usher
1883-84 I Lowthian Bell G A Bell J A Robson
1884-85 I Lowthian Bell G A Bell J A Robson
1885-86 I Lowthian Bell G A Bell F Logan
1886-87 I Lowthian Bell C H Sample F Logan
1887-88 Dr Galbraith H Farrar Alf Patterson
1888-89 Dr Galbraith S Welford Alf Patterson
1889-90 Dr Galbraith H Farrar Alf Patterson
1890-91 Dr Galbraith H Farrar Alf Patterson
1891-92 Dr Galbraith B C Hardy Alf Patterson
1892-93 Dr Galbraith P McAllum Alf Patterson
1893-94 Dr Galbraith C Punter J Brodie
1894-95 Rev W Maddison G C Robinson F Potts
1895-96 Rev W Maddison R M Robinson A Blacklock
1896-97 Rev W Maddison R M Robinson A Blacklock
1897-98 Rev W Maddison R M Robinson W P Ruddock
1898-99 T N Arkle J Brunskill J F Potts
1899-1900 W J Sanderson G Foreman R J Lawson
1900-01 W J Sanderson H Irvine R Kirkup
1901-02 J E Woods G Foreman R Kirkup
1902-03 J E Woods G Foreman R Kirkup
1903-04 Rev W Maddison R H Kirkup T F Forster
1904-05 R J Aynsley R H Kirkup T F Forster
1905-06 R J Aynsley H O Robinson R J Lawson
1906-07 R J Aynsley H O Robinson R J Lawson
1907-08 R J Aynsley H O Robinson R J Lawson
1908-09 R J Aynsley H O Robinson J G Oates
1909-10 R J Aynsley H O Robinson J G Oates
1910-11 R J Aynsley H O Robinson H T Robinson
1911-12 T G Boss H O Robinson H T Robinson
1912-13 T G Boss A Thompson H T Robinson
1913-14 T G Boss G W Fairweather H T Robinson
1914-19 THE FIRST WORLD WAR
1919-20 Lt Col T G Boss W Armstrong H T Robinson
1920-21 Lt Col T G Boss F Johnson H T Robinson
1921-22 Lt Col T G Boss F Johnson H T Robinson
1922-23 Emerson Bainbridge R H Worthington A Elliott
1923-24 Emerson Bainbridge J S Armstrong J S Armstrong
1924-25 R M Robinson G N Wilkinson H M Owen
1925-26 R M Robinson J S Armstrong W Wearmouth
1926-27 R M Robinson J S Armstrong W Wearmouth
1927-28 R M Robinson A D Punter W R Gledson
1928-29 R M Robinson F H Morrison W R Gledson
1929-30 R M Robinson S M Carter W R Gledson
1930-31 R M Robinson R B Horsley W R Doig
1931-32 H O M Robinson S G March W R Doig
1932-33 H O M Robinson S G March W R Doig
1933-34 H O M Robinson H M Kelly W R Doig
1934-35 G P Taylor H M Kelly W R Doig
1935-36 G P Taylor C R Wood W R Doig
1936-37 G P Taylor C R Wood W R Doig
1937-38 G P Taylor C H Errington W R Doig
1938-39 W L Baty C H Errington W R Doig
1939-45 THE SECOND WORLD WAR
1945-46 W L Baty C H Errington G W Robinson
1946-47 W L Baty E A Melling G W Robinson
1947-48 W R Doig H J M Millican H J M Millican
1948-49 M D Oubridge P Gibbons H J M Millican

1949-50 J A Baty D Smith H J M Millican
1950-51 J A Baty J B Raine H J M Millican
1951-52 W Wearmouth J B Raine H J M Millican
1952-53 W L Baty J B Raine H J M Millican
1953-54 N Welch W I Hay J R Veitch
1954-55 E C Hilton J M Smith J R Veitch
1955-56 E C Hilton J M Smith J R Veitch
1956-57 W R Gledson J M Smith J R Veitch
1957-58 P Cooper W Charlton J R Veitch
1958-59 C H Errington G N Smith J R Veitch
1959-60 R Pearson B J G de Zwaan J R Veitch
1960-61 E Dunn F Armstrong J R Veitch
1961-62 G W Robinson D H Campbell N Thom
1962-63 C K Lockerby W Charlton N Thom
1963-64 P C Gibbon T L Hall N Thom
1964-65 A F Davidson R J McLoughlin K S Lockerbie
1965-66 A J Thompson T A Hargrave K S Lockerbie
1966-67 G C B Raine T A Hargrave K S Lockerbie
1967-68 G C B Raine T A Hargrave J M Smith
1968-69 D Smith Jnr M Stokoe J M Smith
1969-70 R C York M Stokoe J M Smith
1970-71 R C York J Rowell J M Smith
1971-72 W Bell J Rowell J M Smith
1972-73 W Bell D F Madsen R C York
1973-74 N Clark D Robinson R C York
1974-75 J M Smith D Robinson R C York
1975-76 J M Smith R M Uttley A W Newton
1976-77 B J G de Zwaan R M Uttley B Colledge
1977-78 D Smith M Young B Colledge
1978-79 R Wood P Dixon B Colledge
1979-80 R Wood C White B Colledge
1980-81 T L Hall C White B Colledge
1981-82 K S Lockerbie R Anderson B Colledge
1982-83 K S Lockerbie B Patrick B Colledge
1983-84 P Southern R Anderson B Colledge
1984-85 N Thom S Gustard B Colledge
1985-86 B Colledge D Johnson E Henderson
1986-87 B Colledge J Curry E Henderson
1987-88 W P Dickinson D Davidson E Henderson
1988-89 J Gray G Smallwood T Farrell
1989-90 J Gray D Briggs T Farrell

Newcastle Gosforth RFC

Year President Captain Secretary
1990-91 J Gray T Roberts T Farrell
1991-92 P L Dobson J Curry P Levinson
1992-93 C Morgan N Frankland P Levinson
1993-94 C Morgan N Frankland P Levinson

Year President Captain Chairman
1994-95 G W Clark R Arnold G S Brown
1995-96 G W Clark S Douglas K S Lockerbie

Newcastle Falcons RFC

Year President Captain Chairman
1996-97 T L Bennett D Ryan Sir John Hall
1997-98 T L Bennett D Ryan Sir John Hall
1998-99 T L Bennett G Armstrong Sir John Hall
1999-2000 T L Bennett G Armstrong D R Thompson

Playing Records

No records are available before 1895-96 and some thereafter are incomplete or are missing.

	P	W	D	F	A	
1895/96	19	10	1	210	101	
1896/97	5	1	2	5	10	(incomplete)
1897/98	No records					
1898/99	7	2	0	33	94	(incomplete)
1899/1900	No records					
1900/01	21	11	2	170	111	
1901/02	16	8	2	95	88	(incomplete)
1902/03	10	4	1	58	74	(incomplete)
1903/04	6	2	0	55	138	(incomplete)
1904/05	5	1	1	29	51	(incomplete)
1905/06	No records					
1906/07	No records					
1907/08	No records					
1908/09	14	1	1	50	247	(incomplete)
1909/10	No records					
1910/11	23	4	1	95	311	
1911/12	No records					
1912/13	26	10	0	204	297	
1913 to '35	No records					
1935/36	21	11	2	190	207	
1936/37	25	9	0	267	310	
1937 to '47	No records					
1947/48	33	11	4	335	332	
1948/49	31	17	3	313	275	
1949/50	37	12	3	277	457	
1950/51	27	18	3	317	166	
1951/52	28	17	2	404	208	
1952/53	31	14	0	302	315	
1953/54	29	8	2	194	288	
1954/55	30	9	2	231	320	
1955/56	36	20	2	277	317	
1956/57	36	20	2	398	249	
1957/58	33	16	2	384	281	
1958/59	30	15	2	226	205	
1959/60	36	29	2	497	158	
1960/61	37	25	3	381	188	
1961/62	37	26	0	483	193	
1962/63	27	22	1	402	116	
1963/64	34	20	2	392	357	
1965/66	38	28	2	447	218	
1967/68	35	22	3	477	269	
1968/69	34	22	2	548	282	
1969/70	36	19	2	343	423	
1970/71	42	30	2	631	348	
1971/72	39	31	0	874	366	
1972/73	42	23	0	910	539	
1973/74	39	31	4	891	333	

	P	W	D	F	A
1974/75	38	30	2	851	286
1975/76	42	36	0	1165	360
1976/77	35	32	1	943	179
1977/78	39	31	0	867	288
1978/79	33	28	1	603	199
1979/80	38	29	0	891	315
1980/81	40	34	1	847	271
1981/82	35	31	0	924	289
1982/83	42	27	3	628	445
1983/84	43	29	3	860	457
1984/85	41	27	0	743	490
1985/86	36	27	1	553	358
1986/87	36	24	1	662	436

League system introduced

Courage League Division 2

	P	W	D	F	A	Pts
1987/88	10	2	1	99	129	17

Tenth – 3 pts for a win, one point for playing

Overall record:

	P	W	D	F	A
1987/88	41	25	1	719	576

Courage League Division 2

	P	W	D	F	A	Pts
1988/89	11	4	0	176	246	8

Tenth – 2 pts for a win

Overall record:

	P	W	D	F	A
1988/89	40	21	1	732	652

Courage League Division 2

	P	W	D	F	A	Pts
1989/90	11	1	1	108	193	3

Bottom – no relegation this season

Overall record:

	P	W	D	F	A
1989/90	40	11	1	526	724

Courage League Division 2

	P	W	D	F	A	Pts
1990/91	12	6	0	169	140	12

Sixth

Overall record:

	P	W	D	F	A
1990/91	34	24	0	722	472

Courage League Division 2

	P	W	D	F	A	Pts
1991/92	12	7	0	371	140	14

Fourth

Overall   record:

	P	W	D	F	A
1991/92	43	35	0	1387	368

Courage League Division 2

	P	W	D	F	A	Pts
1992/93	12	10	0	241	106	20

Champions – promoted

Overall record:

	P	W	D	F	A
1992/93	35	30	2	1001	307

Courage League Division 1

	P	W	D	F	A	Pts
1993/94	18	2	1	190	483	5

Bottom – relegated

Overall record:

	P	W	D	F	A
1993/94	27	8	3	521	572

Courage League Division 2

	P	W	D	F	A	Pts
1994/95	18	8	2	373	281	18

Third

Overall record:

	P	W	D	F	A
1994/95	38	24	2	954	533

Courage League Division 2

	P	W	D	F	A	Pts
1995/96	18	5	1	348	433	11

Eighth

Overall record:

	P	W	D	F	A
1995/96	39	15	2	813	807

Premiership Division 2

	P	W	D	F	A	Pts
1996/97:	22	19	1	1255	346	39

Runners-up – promoted

Overall record:

	P	W	D	F	A
1996/97:	31	23	3	1527	533

Premiership Division 1

	P	W	D	F	A	Pts
1997/98:	22	19	0	645	387	38

Champions

Overall record:

	P	W	D	F	A
1997/98:	36	29	0	1090	533

Premiership Division 1

	P	W	D	F	A	Pts
1998/99	26	14	0	719	639	28

Eighth

Overall record:

	P	W	D	F	A
1998/99:	36	23	1	1065	936

Premiership Division 1

	P	W	D	F	A	Pts
1999/00:	22	6	2	377	630	19

Ninth

Overall record:

	P	W	D	F	A
1999/00:	32	13	2	705	818